THE CUBAN
MISSILE CRISIS
OF
1962

Karl —

Hope you enjoy
this small contribution to
the Kennedy era —

Bill

THE CUBAN MISSILE CRISIS OF 1962

Needless or Necessary

WILLIAM J. MEDLAND

PRAEGER

New York
Westport, Connecticut
London

Library of Congress Cataloging-in-Publication Data

Medland, William J.
  The Cuban missile crisis of 1962.

  Bibliography: p.
  Includes index.
  1. Cuban Missile Crisis, Oct. 1962.
  I. Title.
E841.M43   1988   973.922   87-36025
ISBN 0-275-92844-6 (alk. paper)

Library of Congress Catalog Card Number: 87-36025
ISBN: 0-275-92844-6

First published in 1988

Praeger Publishers, One Madison Avenue, New York, NY 10010
A division of Greenwood Press, Inc.

Printed in the United States of America

The paper used in this book complies with the Permanent
Paper Standard issued by the National Information Standards
Organization (Z39.48—1984).

10 9 8 7 6 5 4 3 2

CONTENTS

Preface	vii
1. THE MISSILE CRISIS: THE NATIONAL CLANDESTINE PHASE, OCTOBER 14–22, 1962	1
2. THE MISSILE CRISIS: THE INTERNATIONAL CONFRONTATION PHASE, OCTOBER 23–NOVEMBER 20, 1962	15
3. THE TRADITIONAL INTERPRETATION: THE PARTICIPANTS' PERSPECTIVE	35
4. THE TRADITIONAL INTERPRETATION: THE OBSERVERS' PERSPECTIVE	63
5. THE REVISIONIST INTERPRETATION: THE RIGHT-WING PERSPECTIVE	81
6. THE REVISIONIST INTERPRETATION: THE LEFT-WING PERSPECTIVE	99
7. THE STRUCTURALIST INTERPRETATION: THE SOVIETOLOGISTS' PERSPECTIVE	127
8. CONCLUSION: ANOTHER INTERPRETATION, ANOTHER PERSPECTIVE	141
Bibliography	149
Index	161
About the Author	169

PREFACE

The emplacement of Soviet missiles in Cuba in October 1962 and the response of the United States to this action thrust the world into its first major nuclear crisis. Because this U.S.-Soviet confrontation seemed to propel the antagonists to the brink of nuclear holocaust, at least in appearance if not also in fact, a number of perspectives have been advanced over the past quarter century regarding this brief but crucial episode in the Cold War. This book is a study of selected historiographical perspectives of the Cuban missile crisis.

Each historiographical chapter is arranged chronologically, according to the publication dates of the interpretations. As far as possible, each chapter of historical perspectives answers several questions. Why did the Soviets emplace missiles in Cuba? Why did the United States respond as it did? What motivated Chairman Nikita S. Khrushchev in his Cuban venture? What motivated President John F. Kennedy in his reaction to the Soviet deployment of missiles in Cuba? Why did the Russians withdraw their missiles? What miscalculations occurred? Who was responsible for the crisis? How well did the President and the Chairman perform during the confrontation? Was the crisis a case of vital interest or nuclear poker? Was the confrontation needless or necessary?

Chapters 1 and 2 describe the national clandestine and international confrontation phases of the missile crisis. While both chapters rely on secondary accounts of the crisis, both heavily utilize the published speeches and messages of the representatives of the United States and the Soviet Union.

Chapters 3 through 7 describe the various perspectives of the interpreters of the missile crisis. The traditional perspective of the American participants is described in Chapter 3, while the traditional interpretation of American observers is presented in Chapter 4. The revisionist interpretations are described in the next two chapters: those of right-wing conservatives in Chapter 5 and those of left-wing liberals in Chapter 6. The perspective of the Sovietologists is described in Chapter 7. The final chapter describes my own reflections.

I was an undergraduate at the University of Notre Dame during the U.S.-Soviet nuclear confrontation of October 1962. I can still remember vividly the enthusiasm and admiration I had for President Kennedy that sunny Sunday following the resolution of the crisis. But events since the crisis, including our politics of escalation in Vietnam and our inability to resolve the proliferation of nuclear weapons, have transformed my perspective.

As no person is an island unto himself, so no manuscript is the product of a single individual. I can only express my deep appreciation to all who have assisted me; their names are too numerous to list. However, I owe a debt of special gratitude to Dwight Hoover, a scholar, author, teacher, and gentleman. He initiated my interest in historiography, and his critique of this material proved invaluable. I also owe a debt of gratitude to my students, whose study of history is enlivened by discussions of historical interpretations. Finally, I am grateful to my wife, Donna, for her patience and support, and to my son, Mark, whose curiosity and inquisitiveness keep me searching for answers.

William J. Medland

1

THE MISSILE CRISIS: THE NATIONAL CLANDESTINE PHASE, OCTOBER 14–22, 1962

Throughout the late summer and early autumn of 1962, Americans became increasingly disturbed at the rapid buildup of Soviet military assistance to the Republic of Cuba. The approach of the congressional elections in November only exacerbated the situation for the Kennedy administration as Republican senators inflamed the domestic scene by calling for an invasion of Cuba.[1] The President held firm to his position that Cuba had a legitimate right to secure defensive weapons, but on September 4 he warned that if there were any evidence of "significant offensive capability either in Cuban hands or under Soviet direction . . . [then] the gravest issues would arise."[2]

The situation increased in intensity as the governments of the United States and the Soviet Union exchanged hostile statements. The Kremlin indicated that the increase of arms and technicians to Cuba was necessitated by the continuous "threats by aggressive imperialist circles with respect to Cuba."[3] The Soviet government stated that the armaments and equipment being sent to Cuba were "solely for defensive purposes" and that since the nuclear weaponry of the Soviet Union was so powerful there was no need "to set up in any other country—Cuba, for instance—the weapons it has for repelling aggression, for a retaliatory blow."[4] A U.S. attack, however, on Cuba or on Soviet ships carrying goods to Cuba would mean war, probably nuclear war.[5]

Replying to the Soviet communiqués and following the photographic discovery of surface-to-air missiles (SAM) in Cuba by reconnaissance flights, President Kennedy stated on September 13 that despite talk in the United States about intervention in Cuba, "unilateral military intervention cannot be either required or justified because of emplacement of Russian defensive weapons."[6] He did issue a stern warning to the Soviet Union:

If at any time the Communist build-up in Cuba were to endanger or interfere with our security in any way, . . . or if Cuba ever attempted to export its aggressive purposes by force or the threat of force . . ., or became an offensive military base of significant capacity for the Soviet Union, then this country will do whatever must be done to protect its own security and that of its allies.[7]

During September President Kennedy increased the schedule of U-2 reconnaissance flights over Cuba. Each of these flights confirmed the emplacement of antiaircraft missiles, but each also confirmed that their slant range of twenty-five miles was clearly no threat to the United States.[8] Thus, despite increasing congressional calls for presidential action, such as those from Senator Kenneth Keating of New York, the Kennedy administration maintained its posture of economic sanctions against Cuba and its position that the Soviet Union had no offensive weapons in Cuba.[9]

As late as Sunday, October 14, Presidential Assistant McGeorge Bundy, appearing on ABC's "Issues and Answers," denied that the Soviets had any offensive military hardware in Cuba. Responding to a question from Edward P. Morgan, Bundy said "there is no present likelihood that the Cubans and the Cuban government and the Soviet government would, in combination, attempt to install a major offensive capability."[10] The security of the United States was not endangered, he said, nor would the administration "permit the situation to develop."[11]

Early Sunday morning, October 14, Air Force Major Rudolf Anderson, Jr. made a U-2 flight over western Cuba.[12] The film aboard the flight was processed and analyzed that evening in routine fashion. By Monday afternoon, however, the photographic interpreters noted that in the San Cristobal area there existed the rude beginnings of a base for medium-range ballistic missiles.[13] This was the beginning of a covert national crisis that would last until October 22, when it would be supplanted by an overt international confrontation.

At 7:00 that evening, General Joseph Carroll, Chief of the Defense Intelligence Agency, notified Roswell Gilpatric, Deputy Secretary of Defense. At 8:30, McGeorge Bundy, special assistant to the President for National Security Affairs, was notified by Ray Cline, Deputy Director of the Central Intelligence Agency (CIA). Dean Rusk, Secretary of State, was notified during his dinner for the West German Foreign Minister by Roger Hilsman, Director of Intelligence and Research in the State Department. Finally, General Maxwell Taylor, Chairman of the Joint Chiefs of Staff, was informed of the situation by General Carroll at a dinner hosted by the general and his wife. Thus, by late evening, most of the key personnel in the military, the State Department, and the Defense Department had been notified. Gilpatric decided not to interrupt Robert McNamara, Secretary of Defense, at the "Hickory Hill University" (seminars conducted at Robert Kennedy's residence in McLean, Virginia), and Bundy decided to wait until morning to notify President Kennedy.[14]

Around 9:00 on Tuesday morning, October 16, Bundy briefed the President on the photographic discovery of Soviet nuclear missiles in Cuba. After reviewing the situation, the President requested Bundy to call a special meeting for 11:45 that morning in the Cabinet Room.[15]

Following his routine schedule of appointments, which included a publicity meeting with astronaut Walter Schirra, Kennedy met at 11:00 with General Marshall Carter, CIA deputy director, to review the photographic intelligence reports. Then at 11:45 the President met with his special group of advisers. This hastily assembled ad hoc committee, which originally nicknamed themselves the "Think Tank" or "War Council" and which on October 22 officially became the Executive Committee (Ex Com) of the National Security Council (NSC), included Secretary of State Rusk, Secretary of Defense McNamara, Deputy Defense Secretary Gilpatric, General Taylor, Presidential Assistant Bundy, CIA Deputy Director Carter (who was replaced by Director John McCone on his return to Washington), Undersecretary of State George Ball, Assistant Secretary of State for Latin American Affairs Edwin Martin, Deputy Undersecretary of State Alexis Johnson, Ambassador-at-Large and Soviet expert Llewellyn Thompson, former Ambassador to Russia Charles Bohlen (who departed for his new ambassadorship to France after the first meeting), Assistant Secretary of Defense Paul Nitze, Attorney General Robert Kennedy, Treasury Secretary Douglas Dillon, and Presidential Special Counsel Theodore Sorensen. Other participants in occasional meetings included Vice-President Lyndon Johnson; Kenneth O'Donnell, Special Assistant to the President; Dean Acheson, former Secretary of State; Adlai Stevenson, Ambassador to the United Nations (U.N.); Donald Wilson, Deputy Director of the United States Information Agency (USIA); and Robert Lovett, former Secretary of Defense and presidential consultant.[16]

In this first unofficial Ex Com meeting, the members assembled were introduced to the photographic evidence as General Carter explained that the Soviet medium-range missiles could reach targets 1,100 miles away; this was sufficient range for the missiles to hit Washington, Dallas, St. Louis, and all Strategic Air Command bases in between. Then, following the Carter report, the committee discussed both the Soviet challenge that the missiles in Cuba presented and the various approaches to a U.S. response. The four possible responses mentioned in the meeting were: (1) do nothing, (2) initiate diplomatic action, (3) bomb or invade Cuba, and (4) implement a blockade. The meeting concluded with the President issuing three directives, which had the effect of: (1) an increase of low-level intelligence flights over Cuba, (2) an intensive survey of all possible courses of action, and (3) strict secrecy on the part of all until a U.S. response could be announced.[17]

After being briefed by Bundy and McCone, the President departed at 9:35 A.M., Wednesday, October 17,. for a campaign tour of Connecticut. The trip had been planned weeks in advance, and the President at the urging of Stevenson had decided not to alter his schedule lest that cause premature alarm.[18]

In the President's absence, the top-level planning group shifted its meetings to George Ball's conference room at the State Department. Dean Acheson joined the War Council as deliberations throughout the day centered on two possible U.S. responses, a blockade and an air strike.[19]

As the meetings were progressing in the State Department, the United States Intelligence Board uncovered new evidence on the Soviet missile buildup in Cuba. The new photographic intelligence now indicated twenty-eight launch pads in various stages of development. Furthermore, for the first time, medium-range missiles were visible. The photographic intelligence also indicated that two kinds of missile sites were being constructed; one type was for the 1,000-mile medium-range ballistic missiles (MRBM), and the other type was for the 2,200-mile intermediate-range ballistic missiles (IRBM). While the intelligence community estimated that it would not be until December before the IRBM sites would be operational, the experts believed that by then forty nuclear warheads could hit targets as far away as Wyoming and Montana. According to the nuclear technicians, such a development would give the Soviet Union a first-strike capability.[20]

President Kennedy's schedule for Thursday morning, October 18, combined the serious and the ceremonial duties of a chief executive, but at 11:00 he found time to meet with his crisis advisers. At this White House meeting, the President was informed that the Intelligence Board estimated that the medium-range nuclear missiles could be operational within eighteen hours. While the Joint Chiefs of Staff started precautionary troop movements, the President again listened to the proponents of the blockade as well as to the proponents of the air strike. For the President and his advisers, the blockade advocates seemed to prevail.[21]

That afternoon, while the Think Tank met in the State Department, the President kept his long-standing two-hour appointment at 5:00 P.M. with Soviet Foreign Minister Andrei Gromyko, who was accompanied by Anatoly Dobrynin, Russian ambassador to the United States. The principal topic of conversation was Berlin, and on this issue Gromyko solemnly promised that the Soviet Union would do nothing about its demands for a free city until after the elections on November

6. Yet the Foreign Minister did indicate that if the United States and the Soviet Union could not reach an agreement on Berlin after the elections, then the Soviets would be compelled to sign a separate peace treaty with East Germany.[22]

Gromyko eventually mentioned the Soviet assistance program to Cuba but not without first protesting against what he referred to as the anti-Cuban campaign in the United States. The Foreign Minister assured the President that the assistance being provided to Cuba "pursued solely the purpose of contributing to the defense capabilities of Cuba . . . ," and he concluded his remarks by saying that if the case were otherwise "the Soviet Government would never become involved in rendering such [offensive military] assistance."[23] The President, while not alluding to the current state of U.S. intelligence, referred to his statement of September 4 in which he emphatically stated that if there were any evidence of "significant offensive capability [in Cuba] . . . [then] the gravest issues would arise."[24] He also reminded Gromyko of the assurances of Nikita Khrushchev and Ambassador Dobrynin that the missiles in Cuba were only antiaircraft weapons incapable of striking U.S. targets.[25]

That evening while Rusk hosted a dinner for Gromyko on the eighth floor of the State Department building, the President's special advisers met a floor below in Ball's conference room. After two hours of deliberations, the exhausted committee members piled into a single limousine for a ride to the White House for a 10:00 P.M. appointment with the President.[26]

The two-hour meeting in the Oval Room confirmed the trend toward a blockade. The President requested Sorensen to start drafting a speech in which he would announce the presence of nuclear missiles in Cuba as well as the measures to be implemented for their immediate removal. General Taylor was given a number of assignments for the Pentagon to execute while the legal advisers for the departments of State, Defense, and Justice began to draft the legal bases for a blockade proclamation.[27]

Early Friday morning, October 19, President Kennedy met for an hour with the Joint Chiefs of Staff, who pleaded for an air strike or an invasion. After listening to their argumentations, the President boarded Air Force One for a campaign trip to the Midwest.[28]

At 10:00 A.M. the War Council reconvened in Ball's conference room. The debate over an air strike versus a blockade was renewed with Bundy preparing the air strike scenario and Alexis Johnson summarizing the blockade argument. The State and Justice departments also presented their legal bases for the blockade. While the debate raged in the conference room, Secretary of Defense McNamara had the Atlantic and Caribbean Commands warned of possible air attacks. Finally, as the evening darkness descended over Washington, the special committee of advisers drifted toward a consensus on the blockade approach as the least provocative response available to the President. Then Sorensen went to the drafting board to write the President's speech.[29]

At 10:00 on Saturday morning, October 20, the Attorney General telephoned the President in Chicago, requesting him to return to Washington. Pierre Salinger, Presidential Press Secretary, announced that the President had a slight cold with a degree of temperature and, therefore, was canceling his campaign trip to return to Washington for some rest as ordered by the White House physician.[30]

Arriving in the Capitol around 1:30 P.M., the President studied Sorensen's blockade speech, and then he joined his group of advisers at 2:30 in the Oval Room for what was convened formally as the 505th meeting of the National Security Council.[31] The two choices presented to the President were either to implement a naval blockade and ascend gradually the ladder of military coercion or to initiate an air strike followed by a full-scale invasion. The President decided upon the blockade, but before his decision became final he wanted to speak with the Air Force Tactical Commander to be certain that a limited surgical air strike on only the missiles and missile sites was not feasible.[32]

During the course of the conversation on possible U.S. action, Ambassador Stevenson suggested that the President should be willing to withdraw the U.S. missiles from Turkey and Italy if the Soviets agreed to withdraw their nuclear missiles from Cuba; likewise, he suggested that the United States should be

willing to surrender its naval base at Guantanamo Bay. Several
of the participants sharply attacked the Stevenson proposal, and
the President forthrightly rejected it.[33]

Before the meeting was adjourned, the timing of the Presidential address to the nation was set for 7:00 P.M., E.S.T.,
Monday, October 22. The time of the speech was called the P-
hour; thus, all activity previous to that hour was referred to as
"P−x hours."[34]

On Sunday morning, October 21, the President met with the
Attorney General, Secretary of Defense, General Taylor, and a
few Air Force officers. The President interrogated Lieutenant
General Walter C. Sweeney, Jr., Commander of the Tactical Air
Command. Responding to a query about the possible outcome
of an air attack on the nuclear missiles in Cuba, Sweeney claimed
that such an attack could destroy 90 percent of the missile sites,
but he conceded that a perfect military air strike was impossi-
ble. The response confirmed the President's decision to implement a naval blockade.[35]

At 2:30 P.M., the National Security Council reconvened and
reviewed the content of the presidential address. Admiral George
W. Anderson, Jr., Navy Chief of Staff, reviewed the plans and
procedures for the blockade. The approaches to the United Nations and to the Organization of American States (OAS) also
were reviewed. Finally, all the plans and machinery that were
to go into effect following the President's speech were reviewed and confirmed.[36]

Monday morning, October 22, the Joint Chiefs of Staff initiated the blockade planning procedures. Missile crews were put
on maximum alert as 162 intercontinental ballistic missiles
(ICBMs) were poised for targets in the Soviet Union; 600 IRBMs
and 250 MRBMs were aimed at other strategic targets. Some
800 nuclear B-47 bombers were dispersed to forty civilian air-
ports, and 550 nuclear-bomb-carrying B-52s took to the air.
Concurrently, the Navy deployed 180 ships to the Caribbean,
including the nuclear carrier *Enterprise*. At the same time, the
Military Air Transport Command flew 7,000 marines to reinforce Guantanamo Bay. To this armada of military power would
soon be added five divisions of the Army (100,000 men) as well
as numerous antiaircraft missile units.[37]

At 3:00 that afternoon, the President met with the full National Security Council, including all the Joint Chiefs of Staff. The President's special advisers were formally constituted as the Executive Committee of the NSC and were to meet henceforth daily at 10:00 A.M. in the Cabinet Room.[38]

At 4:00 P.M. the President met with his full cabinet, and for the first time since the crisis began he informed them of the situation. Then at 5:00, Kennedy joined Rusk, McNamara, and McCone in a special briefing of select congressional leaders, many of whom had been flown back to Washington by Air Force jets from all parts of the country.[39]

At 6:00 that evening, Rusk met with Soviet Ambassador Dobrynin at the State Department and presented him with a copy of the President's speech and a message to Chairman Khrushchev in which the President emphasized that the action he was taking was "the minimum necessary to remove the threat to the security of the nations of this hemisphere."[40] Simultaneously, George Ball and Roger Hilsman briefed forty-six ambassadors from allied countries.[41]

At 7:00 sharp, the President addressed the nation via television and radio:

Good evening, my fellow citizens. This Government, as promised, has maintained the closest surveillance of the Soviet military buildup on the island of Cuba. Within the past week unmistakable evidence has established the fact that a series of offensive missile sites is now in preparation on that imprisoned island. The purpose of these bases can be none other than to provide a nuclear strike capability against the Western Hemisphere.

The characteristics of these new missile sites indicate two distinct types of installations. Several of them include medium-range ballistic missiles capable of carrying a nuclear warhead for a distance of more than 1,000 nautical miles. Each of these missiles, in short, is capable of striking Washington, D.C., the Panama Canal, Cape Canaveral, Mexico City, or any other city in the Southeastern part of the United States, in Central America or in the Caribbean area.

Additional sites not yet completed appear to be designed for intermediate-range ballistic missiles capable of traveling more than twice as far—and thus capable of striking most of the major cities in the Western Hemisphere. . . . In addition, jet bombers, capable of carrying nuclear weapons, are now being uncrated and assembled in Cuba, while the necessary air bases are being prepared.

This urgent transformation of Cuba into an important strategic base—by the presence of these large, long-range, and clearly offensive weapons of sudden mass destruction—constitutes an explicit threat to the peace and security of all the Americas. . . .

But this secret, swift, and extraordinary build-up of Communist missiles . . . for the first time outside of Soviet soil . . . is a deliberately provocative and unjustified change in the status quo which cannot be accepted by this country if our courage and our commitments are ever to be trusted again by either friend or foe.

We will not prematurely or unnecessarily risk the costs of worldwide nuclear war in which even the fruits of victory would be ashes in our mouth—but neither will we shrink from that risk at any time it must be faced.

Acting, therefore, in the defense of our own security and of the entire Western Hemisphere, . . . I have directed the following initial steps to be taken immediately:

First: . . . a strict quarantine on all offensive military equipment under shipment to Cuba is being initiated.

Second: I have directed the continued and increased close surveillance of Cuba and its military build-up.

Third: . . . any nuclear missile launched from Cuba against any nation in the Western Hemisphere [will be considered] as an attack by the Soviet Union on the United States, requiring a full retaliatory response upon the Soviet Union.

Fourth: . . . I have reinforced our base at Guantanamo . . . and ordered additional military units to be on standby alert basis.

Fifth: We are calling tonight for an immediate meeting of . . . the Organization of American States. . . .

Sixth: . . . we are asking tonight an emergency meeting of the [UN] Security Council be convoked. . . .

Seventh and finally: I call upon Chairman Khrushchev to halt and eliminate this clandestine, reckless, and provocative threat to world peace and to stable relations between our two nations.

Our goal is not victory of might but the vindication of right—not peace at the expense of freedom, but both peace and freedom, here in this hemisphere and, we hope, around the world. God willing, that goal will be achieved.[42]

At 7:30 P.M. in New York, Adlai Stevenson delivered the U.S. request for an emergency meeting of the U.N. Security

Council to that month's Chairman, Valerian Zorin, who was also the Soviet Ambassador to the United Nations.[43] Simultaneously in Washington, Edwin Martin briefed the Latin American ambassadors, while Rusk and Hilsman briefed the nonaligned ambassadors. The secret national crisis now had been transformed into an international confrontation.[44]

NOTES

1. Theodore C. Sorensen, *Kennedy* (New York: Harper and Row, 1965; paperback ed., New York: Bantam Books, 1966), p. 754.

2. White House Press Release of September 4, 1962. U.S. Department of State, *Bulletin* 47 (September 24, 1962), 450; cited hereafter as *Bulletin*.

3. Statement of the Soviet Government of September 2, 1962. *Pravda*, September 3, 1962, p. 1; reprinted in *The Current Digest of the Soviet Press* 14 (September 26, 1962), 21; cited hereafter as *Current Digest*.

4. Statement of the Soviet Government of September 11, 1962. *Pravda* and *Izvestia*, September 12, 1962, pp. 1–2; reprinted in *Current Digest* 14 (October 10, 1962), 14.

5. *Ibid.*, 14–15.

6. Statement of President Kennedy of September 13, 1962. *Bulletin* 47 (October 1, 1962), 481–82.

7. *Ibid.*

8. Elie Abel, *The Missile Crisis* (Philadelphia: J. B. Lippincott, 1966), p. 22.

9. Roger Hilsman, *To Move a Nation: The Politics of Foreign Policy in the Administration of John F. Kennedy* (Garden City, N.Y.: Doubleday, 1967), pp. 177–81; Kenneth Keating, "My Advance View of the Cuban Crisis," *Look*, November 3, 1964, pp. 96–106.

10. Edward P. Morgan interview of McGeorge Bundy telecasted on ABC's "Issues and Answers," 3:00 P.M. E.S.T., quoted in Abel, *Missile Crisis*, p. 13; Hilsman, *To Move a Nation*, p. 180.

11. Quoted in Abel, *Missile Crisis*, p. 14; Hilsman, *To Move a Nation*, p. 180.

12. Abel, *Missile Crisis*, p. 27.

13. Sorensen, *Kennedy*, p. 758.

14. Abel, *Missile Crisis*, pp. 28–34; Hilsman, *To Move a Nation*, p. 193; Maxwell D. Taylor, *Swords and Plowshares* (New York: W. W. Norton, 1972), p. 264.

15. Abel, *Missile Crisis*, pp. 43–44; Sorensen, *Kennedy*, p. 759.

16. Robert F. Kennedy, *Thirteen Days: A Memoir of the Cuban Missile Crisis* (New York: W. W. Norton, 1969), p. 30; Sorensen, *Kennedy*, p. 760.

17. Abel, *Missile Crisis*, pp. 47, 50–57; Sorensen, *Kennedy*, pp. 760–62; Hilsman, *To Move a Nation*, pp. 194–96.

18. Abel, *Missile Crisis*, pp. 49, 55; Sorensen, *Kennedy*, p. 773.

19. Abel, *Missile Crisis*, pp. 62–63; Sorensen, *Kennedy*, pp. 773–76.

20. Abel, *Missile Crisis*, p. 59; Sorensen, *Kennedy*, p. 766; Hilsman, *To Move a Nation*, pp. 200–01; Taylor, *Swords and Plowshares*, p. 208.

21. Abel, *Missile Crisis*, pp. 71–73; Sorensen, *Kennedy*, p. 776.

22. Abel, *Missile Crisis*, pp. 74–75; Sorensen, *Kennedy*, p. 778.

23. Statement of Andrei Gromyko to President Kennedy of October 18, 1962. Quoted in Sorensen, *Kennedy*, p. 778; Kennedy, *Thirteen Days*, pp. 40–41.

24. White House Press Release of September 4, 1962. *Bulletin* 47 (September 24, 1962), 450; Sorensen, *Kennedy*, p. 779.

25. Abel, *Missile Crisis*, pp. 75–77; Kennedy, *Thirteen Days*, pp. 40–41.

26. Abel, *Missile Crisis*, pp. 78–81; Sorensen, *Kennedy*, p. 779.

27. Abel, *Missile Crisis*, pp. 81–82; Sorensen, *Kennedy*, pp. 779–80.

28. Abel, *Missile Crisis*, p. 83; Sorensen, *Kennedy*, p. 780.

29. Abel, *Missile Crisis*, pp. 84–90; Sorensen, *Kennedy*, pp. 780–81; Kennedy, *Thirteen Days*, pp. 44–46.

30. Kennedy, *Thirteen Days*, p. 47; Sorensen, *Kennedy*, p. 781.

31. Sorensen, *Kennedy*, p. 782; Abel, *Missile Crisis*, pp. 93–94. Abel agrees with Sorensen on the timing and content of the meeting, but the former indicates that the first official NSC meeting was convened at 2:30 P.M. on Sunday, October 21.

32. Abel, *Missile Crisis*, pp. 93–94; Sorensen, *Kennedy*, p. 782.

33. Kennedy, *Thirteen Days*, p. 49; Abel, *Missile Crisis*, pp. 94–96; Sorensen, *Kennedy*, pp. 784–85. Sorensen agrees with Kennedy and Abel on the proposals, but he does not explicitly identify Stevenson as the originator of them.

34. Sorensen, *Kennedy*, p. 783.

35. Taylor, *Swords and Plowshares*, p. 271; Sorensen, *Kennedy*, p. 786; Abel, *Missile Crisis*, pp. 100–01.

36. Abel, *Missile Crisis*, pp. 106–07; Sorensen, *Kennedy*, pp. 787–90.

37. Henry M. Pachter, *Collision Course: The Cuban Missile Crisis and Coexistence* (New York: Frederick A. Praeger, 1963), pp. 56–57; James E. McSherry, *Khrushchev and Kennedy in Retrospect* (Palo Alto, Calif.: Open-Door Press, 1971), pp. 128–29; Hugh Thomas, *Cuba: The Pursuit of Freedom* (New York: Harper and Row, 1971), p. 1417.

38. Abel, *Missile Crisis*, pp. 115–16; Kennedy, *Thirteen Days*, p. 53.

39. Hilsman, *To Move a Nation*, p. 207–09; Sorensen, *Kennedy*, pp. 790–92.

40. Message of President Kennedy to Chairman Khrushchev of October 22, 1962. *Bulletin* 69 (November 19, 1973), 636.

41. Hilsman, *To Move a Nation*, pp. 207–09; Abel, *Missile Crisis*, pp. 120–21.

42. Address of President Kennedy to the Nation of October 22, 1962. *Bulletin* 47 (November 12, 1962), 715–20.

43. For text of resolution, see *Bulletin* 47 (November 12, 1962), 724.

44. Hilsman, *To Move a Nation*, p. 207; Abel, *Missile Crisis*, pp. 124–25.

2

THE MISSILE CRISIS: THE INTERNATIONAL CONFRONTATION PHASE, OCTOBER 23–NOVEMBER 20, 1962

At 8:00 on Tuesday morning, October 23, the Tass news agency issued an official response by the Soviet Union to the Kennedy announcement of Monday evening. The Soviet government accused the United States of violating international law, of implementing piratical operations, and of provoking nuclear war.[1] As the statement was being announced in the United States, Russian Minister of Defense R. Y. Malinovsky raised to combat readiness all the armed forces of the Soviet Union; concurrently, the Combined Armed Forces of the Warsaw Pact were raised to full military preparedness.[2] Then, shortly before noon in Washington, the State Department received Nikita Khrushchev's reply to President Kennedy's first letter to the Chairman. This first Khrushchev letter of the crisis accused the Kennedy administration of violating the United Nations Charter and international law, and it cautioned the President that his actions could lead to "catastrophic consequences for peace throughout the world."[3]

While the State Department was scrutinizing the statements of Khrushchev and the Soviet government, Dean Rusk was warning the OAS that no country in the Western Hemisphere was "secure either from direct attack or from blackmail."[4] He exhorted the OAS to adopt the resolution drafted by the United States calling for "the immediate dismantling and withdrawal from Cuba of all missiles and other weapons with any offen-

sive capability."[5] Upon Rusk's urging and after consultation
with their respective governments, the OAS adopted the resolution by a vote of 19 to 0 with one abstention by Uruguay,
whose delegate could not contact his government for instructions; the following day, however, Uruguay cast its vote in the
affirmative, making the resolution unanimous.[6]

As the OAS was preparing for a vote on the drafted resolution of the United States, Adlai Stevenson was at the United
Nations introducing the U.S. resolution to the Security Council; the resolution called for the immediate withdrawal of all
missiles and other offensive weapons from Cuba, requested the
dispatchment of a U.N. observer corps to Cuba, and recommended that the United States and the Soviet Union confer to
remove the threat to the security of the Western Hemisphere.
Stevenson called on the Soviet leadership to end its ominous
adventure and to follow the road to peace as contained in the
U.S. resolution.[7] He concluded his remarks by asking that October 23, 1962 "be remembered not as the day when the world
came to the edge of nuclear war but as the day when men
resolved to let nothing thereafter stop them in their quest for
peace."[8]

Garcia-Inchaustegui, Cuban representative in the Security
Council, followed Stevenson's remarks with a denunciation of
the naval quarantine as "an act of war."[9] He requested the
Security Council to act on behalf of Cuba for "the immediate
withdrawal of the aggressive forces of the United States and
the cessation of the illegal, unilateral blockade. . . ."[10]

Soviet Ambassador Zorin thereafter introduced a counter-
esolution condemning the United States and calling upon the
United States, Cuba, and the Soviet Union to enter into negotiations.[11] Zorin claimed that the Soviet Union was only sup-
plying Cuba with military assistance for defensive purposes;
yet the reckless and irresponsible action of the United States to
the Soviet assistance was a step toward "unleashing . . . a world
thermonuclear war."[12]

As the debate raged in the Security Council, the President
met at 6:00 with Ex Com to review the quarantine proclamation.[13] With the support of the North Atlantic Treaty Organization (NATO) and the OAS, Kennedy issued his proclamation

for the "Interdiction of the Delivery of Offensive Weapons to Cuba." The materials prohibited were:

Surface-to-surface missiles; bomber aircraft; bombs, air-to-surface rockets and guided missiles; warheads for any of the above weapons; mechanical or electronic equipment to support or operate the above items; and any other classes of material hereafter designed by the Secretary of Defense for the purpose of effectuating this Proclamation.[14]

After approving the text of the proclamation, the President composed a letter to Khrushchev that was transmitted by the State Department to the American Embassy in Moscow at 6:51 P.M. In this second message to the Chairman, Kennedy urged the Soviets to observe the quarantine that was established legally by the vote of the OAS and that was to go into effect on Wednesday morning, October 24, at 10:00 E.S.T. He admonished Khrushchev to "show prudence and do nothing to allow events to make the situation more difficult to control. . . ."[15]

The President's final act of the day was to shorten the proposed quarantine line by 300 miles. The interception line originally was to be established 800 miles from Cuba, but upon the advice of Ambassador David Ormsby-Gore of Great Britain, President Kennedy ordered the quarantine line shortened to 500 miles so as to give the Soviets more time to contemplate their next decision.[16]

At 10:00 on Wednesday morning, October 24, the quarantine went into effect as sixteen destroyers, three cruisers, an antisubmarine aircraft carrier, and six utility ships with 150 other naval vessels in reserve patrolled the interdiction line.[17] Shortly after the quarantine went into effect, two Russian ships, the *Gagarin* and the *Komiles*, led by a Soviet submarine approached the barrier; as the U.S. carrier *Essex* moved into position for the interception, the Russian ships halted in the water. At 10:30 A.M., the President issued an order in which no ships were to be stopped or intercepted but only shadowed so as to give them every opportunity to reverse their course. As the hours of the day advanced, twenty Russian ships came close to the barrier but none attempted to pass through the line of interdiction. Wednesday thus passed without incident on the high seas.[18]

Although a naval confrontation failed to materialize in the Caribbean, Khrushchev continued to take a tough line against the President's quarantine. In a conversation that afternoon in the Kremlin, the Chairman admitted to William E. Knox, President of Westinghouse Electric International Company, that the Soviet Union had furnished Cuba with nuclear antiaircraft and ballistic missiles for defensive purposes. Khrushchev emphasized that the Soviet Union had a legitimate right to do what it did but that the United States response to the military buildup was piracy, and he would instruct his submarines to sink immediately U.S. naval vessels. The Chairman explained to Knox that he was not interested in destroying the world, but it was up to the United States to determine whether or not everyone would soon meet in hell.[19]

At 9:24 P.M. the State Department received a telegram from Khrushchev transmitted by the American Embassy in Moscow. In rejecting Kennedy's statement that the OAS resolution gave legitimacy to the quarantine, the Chairman denounced the interdiction proclamation as "an act of aggression, · pushing mankind toward the abyss of a world missile-nuclear war."[20] The Chairman indicated that the captains of Soviet vessels bound for Cuba were instructed not to observe the blockade, and he warned that if the United States violated the laws of navigation in international waters, then the Soviet Union would be forced "to take measures . . . necessary and adequate in order to protect [its] rights."[21] Khrushchev concluded his letter by noting: "For this we have all that is necessary."[22]

Late that night President Kennedy composed a reply to Khrushchev's message, which was communicated to the Soviet Embassy in Washington at 1:45 A.M. Kennedy reviewed his statements of September regarding offensive weapons in Cuba and the Soviet assurances that there were no offensive weapons on the island. Reminding the Chairman that it was the Soviet Union that issued the first challenge in the crisis by its emplacement of offensive weapons in Cuba, the President urged Khrushchev to "take the necessary action to permit a restoration of the earlier situation."[23]

The breakfast conversation on Thursday morning, October 25, was provided by Walter Lippmann's column in the *Wash-*

ington Post. Lippmann suggested that there were three ways to get the missiles out of Cuba. One was to invade and occupy Cuba. Another was to institute a total blockade of the island. The third way, the one Lippmann wished to see pursued, was to dismantle the NATO missile base in Turkey in exchange for the Soviet base in Cuba. According to the elder columnist, neither one was of much military value. "The Soviet military base in Cuba is defenseless and the base in Turkey is all but obsolete. The two bases could be dismantled without altering the world balance of power."[24]

As the American people and Soviet personnel stationed in the United States were discussing the Lippmann essay, the first contact between the U.S. navy and a Soviet ship occurred in the Caribbean. At 8:00 A.M. a Russian tanker, the *Bucharest*, reached the interception line. The ship was halted for the purposes of establishing the quarantine and of identification, but it was not boarded. Since the ship was a tanker and its cargo was not on the interdiction list, it was allowed to proceed to Cuba under surveillance of U.S. warships.[25] This was followed by a Pentagon announcement at 11:50 A.M. that "at least a dozen Soviet vessels have turned back because . . . they might have been carrying offensive materials."[26]

Thursday afternoon U.N. Acting Secretary-General U Thant received replies from both Khrushchev and Kennedy regarding his statement to each national leader on Wednesday that the quarantine be suspended for two or three weeks and that the two parties meet to discuss a peaceful solution.[27] Khrushchev accepted the Secretary-General's proposal, saying that it "meets the interest of peace."[28] Kennedy, however, indicated that first there had to be a satisfactory solution to the crisis, because "the existing threat was created by the secret introduction of offensive weapons into Cuba, and the answer lies in the removal of such weapons."[29]

U Thant immediately responded to the Khrushchev and Kennedy letters. He appealed to the Chairman to keep Soviet ships "already on their way to Cuba . . . away from the interception area for a limited time."[30] Likewise, he appealed to the President to have the U.S. naval vessels in the Caribbean "do everything possible to avoid direct confrontation with Soviet ships . . . in order to minimize the risk of any untoward incident."[31]

As U Thant's messages were being sent to the two antagonists in the crisis, the Security Council met in a tension-filled atmosphere as another round of the Stevenson-Zorin talks resumed. In responding to Stevenson's statement that he had incontrovertible evidence of offensive weapons being installed in Cuba, Zorin charged that the United States had no such facts. "Falsity is what the United States has in its hands—false evidence."[32] He accused the United States of deliberately provoking and intensifying the crisis and warned that such "opportunistic steps can lead you to catastrophic consequences for the whole world."[33]

After indicating that he did not have Zorin's talent for obfuscation and distortion, Stevenson addressed the Soviet Ambassador directly:

Do you, Ambassador Zorin, deny that the U.S.S.R. has placed and is placing medium- and intermediate-range missiles and sites in Cuba? Yes or no—don't wait for the translation—yes or no? [The Soviet representative refused to answer.]

You can answer yes or no. You have denied they exist. I want to know if I understand you correctly. I am prepared to wait for my answer until hell freezes over, if that's your decision. And I am also prepared to present the evidence in this room.[34]

Stevenson then set up an easel and exhibited the U.S. photographic intelligence showing the construction of the missile sites. The Security Council adjourned at 7:25 P.M., and it did not reconvene until after the termination of the crisis.[35]

As the Security Council adjourned at 2:25 A.M. Moscow time, those responsible for the Soviet decisions of the crisis week were probably asleep and did not receive the news of Stevenson's photographic presentation until morning. Those individuals who acted as a kind of "Ex Com" of the full Presidium of the Supreme Soviet were Chairman of the Council of Ministers Khrushchev, Chairman of the Presidium Leonid Brezhnev, Secretary of the Central Committee Frol Kozlov, and First Deputy Chairman of the Council of Ministers Aleksey Kosygin. They were joined on occasion by other members of the Council, including Anastasy Mikoyan, Dmitri Polyansky, and Mikhail Suslov.[36]

Early Friday morning, October 26, as the sun rose over the sparkling blue waters of the Caribbean, a navy party from the U.S.S. *Joseph P. Kennedy, Jr.* boarded for the first time a Soviet supply vessel. The *Marucla* was a Panamanian-owned, American-built Liberty ship that was registered in Lebanon and bound for Cuba under a Soviet charter from the port of Riga on the Baltic Sea. The boarding occurred without incident, and the *Marucla* was permitted through the quarantine barrier since its cargo was not on the contraband list.[37]

Meanwhile in Moscow that day's edition of *Pravda* appeared on the newsstands with the headline "Reason Must Triumph!" The leading editorial stated that the Soviet Union should be willing to suspend shipments of arms to Cuba for an American willingness to suspend the blockade. The editorial emphasized the need for reason to prevail in order to avoid a military catastrophe. "Washington must realize," the editor explained, "that this acutely aggravated situation can push the world into the abyss of war."[38] Another writer in the same paper suggested that the crisis situation called for statesmen as never before "to display cool-headedness and discretion."[39]

That afternoon U Thant received replies to his October 25 messages to Khrushchev and Kennedy. The Chairman indicated that the captains of Soviet vessels bound for Cuba had been ordered to stay clear of the blockade barrier.[40] Likewise, the President informed U Thant that the United States would do everything possible to avoid a direct confrontation at sea if the Soviet ships stayed away from the area of interception. Kennedy, however, emphasized that the missiles in Cuba had to be "withdrawn in order to end the threat to peace."[41]

In Washington, Ex Com was meeting all day to discuss the new intelligence evidence from low-level reconnaissance flights over Cuba the previous day. The rapid development of missiles and MRBM launch facilities was continuing. Even the construction of the intermediate-range ballistic missile sites was progressing unabated.[42]

Ex Com began to make secret contingency plans for an air

strike and an invasion of Cuba. Don Wilson of the USIA was authorized that morning to print 5 million leaflets in Spanish explaining the reasons why the United States had been forced to execute military operations. The Department of Defense ordered antiaircraft missiles into Key West, Florida, and the State Department made preparations for the establishment of a civil government in Cuba after the invasion.[43]

At noon that Friday, Lincoln White, a State Department spokesman, briefed the press on the continuing developments of the crisis. White announced that the work on the missile sites was proceeding without interruption; he then added without presidential authorization that "further action will be justified."[44] The remark immediately initiated rumors that an air strike or an invasion was imminent.[45]

That afernoon at 1:30, John Scali, State Department correspondent for ABC, received an urgent telephone call from Aleksander Fomin, a Soviet Embassy counselor, who suggested that the two meet immediately at the Occidental Restaurant.[46] There Fomin presented Scali with a proposal: "Bases would be dismantled under United Nations supervision and Castro would plege not to accept offensive weapons of any kind, ever, in return for a U.S. pledge not to invade Cuba."[47]

After conferring with Hilsman and Rusk at the State Department, Scali met Fomin at 7:30 P.M. at the Statler Hotel. The news correspondent indicated that the United States government saw "real possibilities" in the proposal, but he indicated that "time is very urgent."[48] Fomin asked Scali if the information he had came from the highest sources in the government, and Scali indicated that it did. Then Scali inquired as to whether the Soviet Union would promise not to ship offensive weapons to Cuba again. Fomin replied in the affirmative, but he quickly inquired as to whether it would be possible "to have the United Nations inspectors also check the American military bases in Florida to make sure that there would be no invasion of Cuba."[49] Scali replied that he could not answer for his government, but he explained that such a proposal would complicate the situation terribly. Fomin then departed hurriedly, leaving a five dollar bill for a thirty-cent check.[50]

At 6:00 P.M. the State Department began receiving a transmission from the American Embassy in Moscow. What was being cabled was a secret letter from Khrushchev to Kennedy. Because of the time involved in translating the Russian language and then encoding the message for transmission, the letter was not received in its entirety until about 9:00.[51] The translation given to the President stated:

We must not succumb to intoxication and petty passions, regardless of whether elections are impending. . . . These are all transient things, but if indeed war should break out, then it would not be in our power to stop it, for such is the logic of war.

. . . All the means located there [in Cuba are] . . . solely for the purposes of defense, and we have sent them to Cuba at the request of the Cuban Government.

You have now proclaimed piratical measures, which were employed in the Middle Ages, when ships . . . were attacked. . . . Our vessels . . . will soon enter the zone which your navy is patrolling. I assure you that these vessels . . . are carrying the most innocent peaceful cargoes.

Consequently, Mr. President, let us show good sense. I assure you that on those ships . . . there are no weapons at all. The weapons which are necessary for the defense of Cuba are already there.

. . . If you stop the vessels . . . that would be piracy. . . . one cannot legalize lawlessness. If this were permitted, then there would be no peace. . . . We should then be forced to put into effect the necessary measures . . . to protect our interests. . . .

If assurances were given by the President . . . that the USA itself would not participate in an attack on Cuba . . . [and] if you would recall your fleet, [then] this would immediately change everything. Then, too, the question of armaments would disappear. . . .

Let us therefore show statesmanlike wisdom. I propose: we, for our part, will declare that our ships, bound for Cuba, will not carry any kind of armaments. You would declare that the United States will not invade Cuba. . . . Then the necessity for the presence of our military specialists in Cuba would disappear.

. . . Mr. President, we and you ought not to pull on the ends of the rope in which you have tied the knot of war, because the more the two of us pull, the tighter that knot will be tied. And a moment may come when that knot will be tied so tight that even he who tied it will not have the strength to untie it, and then it will be necessary to cut that knot.

Consequently, if there is no intention to tighten that knot and thereby to doom the world to the catastrophe of thermonuclear war, then let us not only relax the forces pulling on the ends of the rope, [but] let us [also] take measures to untie that knot. We are ready for this.[52]

At 10:00 P.M. the Executive Committee convened to examine the Khrushchev proposal. The participants decided that the State Department should analyze the letter and prepare a response. Secretary Rusk therefore requested Hilsman and others in the Bureau of Intelligence and Research to prepare an analysis of a reply to the Khrushchev cable and the Scali-Fomin exchange.[53]

While Hilsman and company labored into the night, the Federal Bureau of Investigation noted that Soviet personnel in New York apparently were preparing to destroy sensitive documents. According to J. Edgar Hoover, such action was being undertaken in anticipation of U.S. military action against Cuba or the Soviet Union.[54]

Ex Com met at 10:00 on Saturday morning, October 27, in an atmosphere filled with optimism generated by the Khrushchev response of the previous evening, but that optimism was shattered at 10:17 when the American Embassy began transmitting a second Russian proposal that was being broadcast over Moscow radio.[55] The new letter from Khrushchev was markedly different in style than the initial message of the night of October 26. The new message to President Kennedy was a formal, bureaucratic-type communication in which the Chairman addressed the President thusly:

You are worried over Cuba . . . because it lies 90 miles across the sea from the shores of the United States. However, Turkey lies next to us. Our sentinels are pacing up and down and watching each other. Do you believe that you have the right to demand security for your country and the removal of such weapons that you qualify as offensive, while not recognizing this right for us? You have stationed devastating rocket weapons, which you call offensive, in Turkey literally right next to us.

This is why I make this proposal: We agree to remove those weapons from Cuba which you regard as offensive weapons. We agree to do this and to state this commitment in the United Nations. Your representatives will make a statement to the effect that the United States, on its part, . . . will evacuate its analogous weapons from Tur-

key. After this, representatives of the U.N. Security Council could
control on-the-spot the fulfillment of these commitments.

   . . . The Soviet Government gives a solemn pledge . . . not to
invade Turkey. . . . The U.S. Government will make the same statement in the Security Council with regard to Cuba. It will declare . . .
not to invade . . . Cuba. . . .

The weapons on Cuba . . . are in the hands of Soviet officers.
Therefore any accidental use of them whatsoever to the detriment of
the United States of America is excluded.

   . . . The greatest pleasure of all the peoples would be an announcement on our agreement, on nipping in the bud the conflict that
has arisen. I attach a great importance to such understanding because
it might be a good beginning and, specifically, facilitate a nuclear test
ban agreement.[56]

The members of Ex Com were bewildered by the new communiqué, but their bewilderment soon turned to shock as they
were informed that the photographic intelligence gathered the
previous day indicated that work was progressing rapidly on
the missile sites. Permanent nuclear warhead storage bunkers
and troop barracks were still being constructed. Ex Com also
was informed that morning that a Soviet ship had detached
itself from the others outside the quarantine line and was approaching the interception barrier on its seaward course to Cuba.
Ex Com could only wonder if the Soviets intended to test U.S.
determination by a confrontation at sea.[57]

The worst news quickly followed. A surface-to-air missile had
shot down an American U-2 plane and had killed the pilot,
Major Rudolph Anderson, Jr., the individual whose U-2 flight
of Sunday, October 14, had discovered the Soviet missiles in
Cuba.[58] What did this mean, pondered Ex Com. Had not the
most recent message of Khrushchev explicitly stated that the
weapons in Cuba were under Soviet control and that there would
be no accidental use of them?

The Joint Chiefs of Staff who had joined the Ex Com morning meeting urged the President to retaliate to this incident by
initiating an air strike followed by an invasion of Cuba.[59] The
President hesitated, but he did order the U.S. armed forces to
be put on full alert worldwide and authorized the largest invasion force mounted since World War II to be assembled in

Florida.[60] Later that day, the President ordered twenty-four troop carrier squadrons of the Air Force Reserve (14,000 men) to active duty for the invasion.[61]

Early that afternoon as Hilsman was delivering to the White House the State Department's response to Khrushchev's letter of Friday night, a "Dr. Strangelove" type incident was developing in the evening skies over the Soviet Union. A U-2 pilot on a routine air sampling mission between Alaska and the North Pole accidentally picked the wrong star for his return flight and soon found himself within Soviet air space. As U.S. fighter planes from Alaska scrambled to escort the U-2 pilot home, a host of Soviet fighters took to the air for the interception.[62] Although a confrontation was avoided ever so narrowly, Khrushchev wondered whether the incident was a prelude to U.S. nuclear bomber attack, especially since the United States was cognizant of the fact that the Soviet armed forces had been put into full combat readiness.[63]

At the request of Secretary Rusk, Scali met Fomin again at the Statler Hotel at 4:15 P.M. The ABC correspondent asked Fomin what had transpired between the two Khrushchev messages of Friday night and Saturday morning. Fomin explained that because of poor communications the second message of Saturday had been drafted before this response of favorable U.S. reaction to the Friday proposal reached Moscow. While he claimed he had no prior knowledge of the proposal broadcast by Moscow radio, Fomin stated that he saw nothing new in the message because Lippmann had mentioned it in his newspaper column on Thursday, October 25. Scali then exploded and told Fomin that a Turkish-Cuban deal was totally unacceptable, but a solution was urgent as time was critically short.[64]

Ex Com read Scali's memo of his exchange with Fomin, and then the White House issued a press release announcement that the United States had received inconsistent and conflicting Russian proposals within the past twenty-four hours. While not rejecting outright the Soviet proposal for removing U.S. missiles in Turkey, the announcement emphatically stressed that the most urgent requirement before negotiations could proceed was to render the offensive missiles in Cuba inoperable; the

United States and its allies then would be willing to discuss arms limitation and the security of nations outside the Western Hemisphere.[65]

Ex Com, meanwhile, led by the Attorney General decided to utilize the "Trollope Ploy."[66] Robert Kennedy suggested that the President respond only to the first Khrushchev cable and to the Scali-Fomin exchange of Friday; no specific mention was to be made of the second Khrushchev proposal of Saturday morning. The President accepted this politically diplomatic maneuver and had Sorenson and his brother compose the message.[67]

Shortly after 8:00 that evening, the State Department transmitted the President's letter to the American Embassy in Moscow for delivery to the Soviet Foreign Ministry. The President acknowledged Khrushchev's letter of October 26 and stated that he welcomed the Chairman's desire for a prompt solution to the crisis. However, the President explained, the first requisite for a solution was that work on the missile sites cease and that the offensive missiles be rendered inoperable under United Nations arrangements. Then he continued:

As I read your letter, the key elements of your proposals—which seem generally acceptable as I understand them—are as follows: (1) You would agree to remove these weapons systems from Cuba under appropriate United Nations observation and supervision [which had been mentioned only by Fomin]; and undertake, with suitable safeguards, to halt the further introduction of such weapons systems into Cuba. (2) We, on our part, would agree—upon the establishment of adequate arrangements through the United Nations to ensure the carrying out and continuation of these commitments—(a) to remove promptly the quarantine measures now in effect and (b) to give assurances against an invasion of Cuba.[68]

The President concluded his message with a stern warning:

The continuation of this threat, or a prolonging of this discussion concerning Cuba by linking these problems to the broader questions of European and world security, would surely lead to an intensification of the Cuban crisis and a grave risk to the peace of the world.[69]

After the presidential message was released to the news media, the President dispatched his brother with a copy of the

letter to Ambassador Dobrynin. The Attorney General emphasized to Dobrynin that it was essential that the missile bases be
removed immediately; if the Soviet Union did not remove the
nuclear bases, then the United States would be forced to remove them. He further explained that if the Soviet Union believed it necessary to take retaliatory measures, then there would
be not only dead Americans but dead Russians as well. As
Kennedy was leaving, he indicated that time was running out
and it was imperative that the United States have a Soviet answer by the next day.[70]

At 9:00 P.M. the Executive Committee met for its third and
final session of this climactic Saturday. The participants again
discussed previously enumerated responses to the crisis, such
as adding petroleum, oil, and lubricants to the quarantine lists,
executing an air strike, or intitiating an invasion.[71] The President, however, decided to wait until the next morning before
making any decision. While the President hoped for a peaceful
solution to the crisis, the expectation was that there would be
a military confrontation by Tuesday if not by the next morning.[72]

The sun dawned on Sunday, October 28, full of the radiance
of a robust autumn day, strangely out of line with the macabre
expectations of the members of the Executive Committee and
the President of the United States. At precisely 9:00, Moscow
radio began broadcasting a letter from Khrushchev to Kennedy.[73] The Chairman in his fifth message to the President in
seven days stated:

In order to eliminate as rapidly as possible the conflict which endan-
gers the course of peace, to give an assurance to all people who crave
peace, and to reassure the American people who, I am certain, also
want peace, as do the people of the Soviet Union, the Soviet Government . . . has given a new order to dismantle the arms which you
describe as offensive, and to crate and return them to the Soviet Union.

I regard with respect and trust the statement you made in your
message of October 27, 1962, that there would be no attack, no invasion of Cuba, not only on the part of the United States, but also on
the part of other nations of the Western Hemisphere, as you said in
your same message. Then the motives which induced us to render

assistance of such a kind to Cuba disappear. It is for this reason that we instructed our officers . . . to take appropriate measures to discontinue construction of the aforementioned facilities, to dismantle them, and to return them to the Soviet Union. . . . We are prepared to reach agreement to enable United Nations Representatives to verify the dismantling of these means. Thus, in view of the assurances you have given and our instructions on dismantling, there is every condition for eliminating the present conflict.[74]

Without waiting for the official cable to be received in the State Department, the President responded to Khrushchev's broadcast message that afternoon. After indicating that developments in the crisis were approaching a point where events could have become unmanageable, Kennedy stated:

I consider my letter to you of October twenty-seventh and your reply of today as firm understandings on the part of both our governments which should be promptly carried out. I hope that the necessary measures can at once be taken through the United Nations . . . so that the United States in turn will be able to remove the quarantine measures now in effect.

We must devote urgent attention to disarmament. . . . I think we should give priority to questions relating to the proliferation of nuclear weapons, on earth and in outer space, and to the great effort for a nuclear test ban.[75]

As the radiance of the sun faded from the skies over the Potomac on that golden autumn afternoon, so did the crisis of the missiles of October.

On November 1, Prime Minister Fidel Castro announced that Cuba would not permit U.N. inspection of its territory.[76] President Kennedy responded the next day, indicating that the United States would continue its aerial surveillance of Cuba as well as the quarantine.[77]

On November 8 the Defense Department announced that the nuclear equipment on the island of Cuba was being removed by the Soviets and that U.S. reconnaissance planes with the cooperation of the Russian vessels were verifying the removal of the missiles.[78] Then on November 20, after receiving assurances from Chairman Khrushchev that all of the IL-28 bombers in Cuba would be withdrawn within thirty days and after verifying that the missiles and their associated equipment had been removed, President Kennedy announced the termination of the naval quarantine.[79] Thus, for the first time in a month, the international waters of the Caribbean were reopened to worldwide shipping. Normalcy had returned to the Caribbean Sea and to U.S.-Soviet relations.

NOTES

1. Statement of the Soviet Government of October 23, 1962. *Pravda* and *Izvestia*, October 24, 1962, p. 1; reprinted in *The Current Digest of the Soviet Press* 14 (November 21, 1962), 4; cited hereafter as *Current Digest*; reprinted in *New York Times*, October 24, 1962, p. 20.

2. Statement of the USSR Council of Ministers of October 23, 1962. *Pravda* and *Izvestia*, October 24, 1962, p. 1; reprinted in *Current Digest* 14 (November 21, 1962), 4.

3. Message of Chairman Khrushchev to President Kennedy of October 23, 1962. U.S. Department of State, *Bulletin* 69 (November 19, 1973), 636; cited hereafter as *Bulletin*. All citations of Chairman Khrushchev's letters to President Kennedy are from the informal translations made at the time of communications and presented to the President; formal translations were prepared subsequently.

4. Statement of Secretary Rusk to the OAS of October 23, 1962. *Bulletin* 47 (November 12, 1962), 721.

5. Resolution of the OAS Organ of Consultation of October 23, 1962. *Bulletin* 47 (November 12, 1962), 723.

6. *Ibid.*, 722.

7. Statement of Ambassador Stevenson to the U.N. Security Council of October 23, 1962. *Bulletin* 47 (November 12, 1962), 733–34.

8. *Ibid.*, 734.

9. Statement of Garcia-Inchaustegui to the U.N. Security Council of October 23, 1962. U.S. Department of State, *American Foreign Policy: Current Documents, 1962* (Washington, D.C.: U.S. Government Printing Office, 1966), document III-63, p. 418; cited hereafter as *Current Documents*.

10. *Ibid.*, p. 419.

11. Statement of Ambassador Zorin to the U.N. Security Council of October 23, 1962. *Current Documents* III-64, pp. 419–20.

12. *Ibid.*, p. 419.

13. Theodore C. Sorensen, *Kennedy* (New York: Harper and Row, 1965; paperback ed., New York: Bantam Books, 1966), p. 798; Robert F. Kennedy, *Thirteen Days: A Memoir of the Cuban Missile Crisis* (New York: W. W. Norton, 1969), p. 60.

14. Presidential Proclamation of October 23, 1962, on the Interdiction of the Delivery of Offensive Weapons to Cuba. *Bulletin* 47 (November 12, 1962), 717.

15. Message of President Kennedy to Chairman Khrushchev of October 23, 1962. *Bulletin* 69 (November 19, 1973), 637.

16. Dan Caldwell, "A Research Note on the Quarantine of Cuba, October 1962," *International Studies Quarterly* 22 (December 1978), 625–33; Kennedy, *Thirteen Days*, p. 67.

17. Sorensen, *Kennedy*, p. 798.

18. Kennedy, *Thirteen Days*, pp. 68–72.

19. William E. Knox, "Close-Up of Khrushchev During a Crisis," *New York Times Magazine*, November 18, 1962, pp. 32, 128–29.

20. Message of Chairman Khrushchev to President Kennedy of October 24, 1962. *Bulletin* 69 (November 19, 1973), 638.

21. *Ibid.*

22. *Ibid.*

23. Message of President Kennedy to Chairman Khrushchev of October 25, 1962. *Bulletin* 69 (November 19, 1973), 639.

24. *Washington Post*, 25 October 1962. Quoted in Elie Abel, *The Missile Crisis* (Philadelphia: J. B. Lippincott, 1966), p. 158; Graham T. Allison, *Essence of Decision: Explaining the Cuban Missile Crisis* (Boston: Little, Brown, 1971), p. 43.

25. *New York Times*, October 26, 1962, p. 17; Roger Hilsman, *To Move a Nation: The Politics of Foreign Policy in the Administration of John F. Kennedy* (Garden City, N.Y.: Doubleday, 1967), p. 212.

26. Pentagon Statement of Arthur Sylvester of October 25, 1962. Quoted in Abel, *Missile Crisis*, p. 163.

27. Messages of U.N. Secretary-General U Thant to Chairman Khrushchev and President Kennedy of October 24, 1962. *Current Documents* III-66, 67, pp. 422–23.

28. Message of Chairman Khrushchev to U.N. Secretary-General U Thant of October 25, 1962. *Current Documents* III-69, p. 425.

29. White House Press Release of October 25, 1962. *Bulletin* 47 (November 12, 1962), 740.

30. Message of U.N. Secretary-General U Thant to Chairman Khrushchev of October 25, 1962. *Current Documents* III-70, p. 425.

31. Message of U.N. Secretary-General U Thant to President Kennedy of October 25, 1962. *Current Documents* III-71, p. 426.

32. Statement of Ambassador Zorin to the U.N. Security Council of October 25, 1962. *Current Documents* III-73, p. 431.

33. *Ibid.*, 432.

34. Statement of Ambassador Stevenson to the U.N. Security Council of October 25, 1962. *Bulletin* 47 (November 12, 1962), 738.

35. *Ibid.*, 739–40.

36. Michael Tatu, *Power in the Kremlin: From Khrushchev to Kosygin*, trans. Helen Katel (New York: The Viking Press, 1969), pp. 272, 549–54.

37. *New York Times*, October 27, 1962, p. 6; Kennedy, *Thirteen Days*, pp. 81–83.

38. *Pravda*, October 26, 1962, p. 1; reprinted in *Current Digest* 14 (November 21, 1962), 8.

39. *Pravda*, October 26, 1962, p. 5; reprinted in *Current Digest* 14 (November 21, 1962), 10.

40. Message of Chairman Khrushchev to U.N. Secretary-General U Thant of October 25, 1962; delivered on October 26. *Current Documents* III-79, p. 437.

41. Message of President Kennedy to U.N. Secretary-General U Thant of October 25, 1962; delivered on October 26. *Current Documents* III-78, p. 436.

42. White House Press Release of October 26, 1962. *Bulletin* 47 (12 November 1962), 740–41.

43. Kennedy, *Thirteen Days*, pp. 85–86; Sorensen, *Kennedy*, p. 802; Abel, *Missile Crisis*, p. 177.

44. Quoted in Sorensen, *Kennedy*, p. 802; Abel, *Missile Crisis*, p. 175.

45. Sorensen, *Kennedy*, p. 802.

46. Hilsman, *To Move a Nation*, p. 217; Abel, *Missile Crisis*, p. 177.

47. Memo of John Scali to Roger Hilsman of October 26, 1962. Quoted in Pierre Salinger, *With Kennedy* (Garden City, N.Y.: Doubleday, 1966), p. 274; Hilsman, *To Move a Nation*, p. 217.

48. Memo of Secretary Rusk to John Scali of October 26, 1962. Quoted in Hilsman, *To Move a Nation*, p. 218; Salinger, *With Kennedy*, p. 275.

49. Memo of John Scali to Secretary Rusk of October 26, 1962. Quoted in Salinger, *With Kennedy*, p. 275; Hilsman, *To Move a Nation*, p. 218.

50. Hilsman, *To Move a Nation*, p. 219.

51. Message of Chairman Khrushchev to President Kennedy of October 26, 1962. *Bulletin* 69 (November 19, 1973), 640–43.

52. *Ibid.*

53. Hilsman, *To Move a Nation*, p. 219; Kennedy, *Thirteen Days*, p. 90; Abel, *Missile Crisis*, p. 185.

54. Kennedy, *Thirteen Days*, p. 93.

55. Hilsman, *To Move a Nation*, p. 220; James McSherry, *Khrushchev and Kennedy in Retrospect* (Palo Alto, Calif.: Open-Door Press, 1971), p. 138.

56. Message of Chairman Khrushchev to President Kennedy of October 27, 1962. *Bulletin* 69 (November 19, 1973), 646–47.

57. Sorensen, *Kennedy*, p. 803; Hilsman, *To Move a Nation*, p. 220.

58. Kennedy, *Thirteen Days*, p. 97; Hilsman, *To Move a Nation*, p. 220; Sorensen, *Kennedy*, p. 804.

59. Kennedy, *Thirteen Days*, pp. 96–97.

60. Sorensen, *Kennedy*, p. 804.

61. Kennedy, *Thirteen Days*, p. 109.

62. Hilsman, *To Move a Nation*, p. 221; Sorensen, *Kennedy*, p. 804; Abel, *Missile Crisis*, p. 195.

63. Message of Chairman Khrushchev to President Kennedy of October 28, 1962. *Bulletin* 47 (November 12, 1962), 745.

64. Memo of John Scali to Secretary Rusk of October 27, 1962. Quoted in Salinger, *With Kennedy*, pp. 277–78; Hilsman, *To Move a Nation*, pp. 222–23.

65. White House Press Release of October 27, 1962. *Bulletin* 47 (November 12, 1962), 741.

66. The term comes from recurrent scenes in Anthony Trollope's novels in which a girl interprets the squeeze of her hand as a marriage proposal.

67. Kennedy, *Thirteen Days*, pp. 101–02; Sorensen, *Kennedy*, pp. 805–06.

68. Message of President Kennedy to Chairman Khrushchev of October 27, 1962. *Bulletin* 69 (November 19, 1973), 649.

69. *Ibid.*, 650.

70. Kennedy, *Thirteen Days*, pp. 107–09; Sorensen, *Kennedy*, p. 806; Hilsman, *To Move a Nation*, p. 224.

71. Sorensen, *Kennedy*, p. 806; Abel, *Missile Crisis*, pp. 201–02.

72. Kennedy, *Thirteen Days*, p. 109; Sorensen, *Kennedy*, pp. 806–07.

73. Abel, *Missile Crisis*, pp. 203–04; Sorensen, *Kennedy*, p. 807.

74. Message of Chairman Khrushchev to President Kennedy of October 28, 1962. *Bulletin* 69 (November 19, 1973), 650–51.

75. Message of President Kennedy to Chairman Khrushchev of October 28, 1962. *Bulletin* 69 (November 19, 1973), 654–55. On August 5, 1963, a treaty banning all nuclear tests except those held underground was signed in Moscow by Rusk, Gromyko, and Lord Home of Great Britain.

76. Statement of Prime Minister Castro via Havana television of November 1, 1962. *Current Documents* III-96, p. 450.

77. White House Press Release of November 2, 1962. *Bulletin* 47 (November 12, 1962), 762.

78. Department of Defense Press Release of November 8, 1962. Reprinted in the *New York Times*, November 9, 1962, p. 3.

79. Statement of President Kennedy on Cuba of November 20, 1962. *Bulletin* 47 (December 10, 1962), 874–75.

3

THE TRADITIONAL INTERPRETATION: THE PARTICIPANTS' PERSPECTIVE

The traditional interpretation of the Cuban missile crisis is fostered both by the participants in the Kennedy administration and by contemporary observers of the nuclear confrontation. The accounts of the former, however, comprise most of the historical literature written on the subject from the traditionalist perspective. The former members of the Kennedy administration, as a group, not only are the most prolific writers on the Cuban missile crisis but also are the staunchest advocates for a traditional interpretation.

The traditionalists hold that intelligence agencies in both the United States and the Soviet Union grossly miscalculated each other's actions. According to the traditionalists, U.S. intelligence experts believed that Soviet foreign policy was too cautious and restrained to permit the emplacement of ballistic missiles in a communist satellite country, especially in a nation as unstable as Cuba. Soviet intelligence likewise miscalculated the determined U.S. response to the emplacement of Soviet missiles in the Western Hemisphere.

According to traditionalists, President Kennedy was forced to respond by necessity to the nuclear offensive missiles in Cuba because such represented a Soviet threat to alter the balance of power either in actuality or in appearance. The U.S. response in the form of quarantine, reinforced by U.S. conventional military superiority in the Western Hemisphere and overall nuclear superiority, was superb in that it exerted maximum pressure on the Soviet Union while incurring the minimum risk of war.

The traditionalists also claim that President Kennedy responded magnificently to the crisis. The President acted calmly, rationally, and responsibly throughout the confrontation. He was always in control of himself and of events; as such, he responsibly and objectively exercised the power at his command to terminate successfully the crisis via the removal of Soviet offensive nuclear missiles from Cuba. Furthermore, President Kennedy's management and resolution of the crisis initiated a thaw in the Cold War, which led to détente evidenced both by the installation of a "hot line" between the White House and the Kremlin and by the signing of a nuclear test ban treaty.

One of the earliest traditionalist versions of the Cuban missile crisis by a high-level administrator in the Kennedy administration and by a key participant in the crisis deliberations was Theodore C. Sorensen's *Kennedy* (1965).[1] According to Sorensen, Special Counsel to the President, the Executive Committee of the National Security Council, of which Sorensen was a member, considered five theories as possible reasons for the Soviet emplacement of missiles in Cuba: (1) Cold War politics to test U.S. resolve, (2) a diversion to cover a Soviet move on Berlin, (3) a defense of Cuba to strengthen the Soviet Union in a contest with the People's Republic of China, (4) a leverage for bargaining for the withdrawal of U.S. overseas bases, and (5) a means of altering the strategic balance of power.[2] President Kennedy regarded the third and fifth reasons as providing likely but insufficient motives for what he considered a drastic and dangerous departure from traditional Soviet foreign and military policies. While all the reasons tend to interrelate, the President gave primary credence to the first reason because he believed that the secrecy and duplicity of the whole Soviet effort was designed to present the United States with a fait accompli to which the United States, from the Russian perspective, would not respond. Yet, whatever the reason, the President did believe that if the Soviet effort were successful, it would change politically and materially the balance of power in the world arena.[3] Unfortunately, Sorensen does not explain why the

President rejected the second and fourth reasons; he also fails to make it perfectly clear whether Kennedy considered the Soviet action to be only a challenge to U.S. national resolve or a personal challenge to himself as President.

According to the traditionalist theory of Cold War politics, Khrushchev believed that the United States would be timid and would not risk nuclear war over the missiles in Cuba. The United States then would appear weak and irresolute, causing its allies to doubt U.S. resolve. Therefore, the Soviet Union could move more easily into West Berlin using the missiles in Cuba as blackmail.[4]

The second theory holds that the missiles in Cuba were a diverting trap. This theory hypothesizes that if the United States attacked Cuba, then the United Nations, the U.S. allies, and the Latin American countries would be in such a disarray that Khrushchev in the confusion would move swiftly into West Berlin.[5]

According to the Cuban defense theory, Khrushchev considered Cuba, as a Soviet satellite, to be essential both in his drive for expansion and in his contest for world communist leadership with Red China. Thus, the missiles were emplaced in Cuba to prevent an invasion from the United States or from hostile Latin American states.[6]

The fourth theory is that the missiles in Cuba were to provide Khrushchev with a leverage for bargaining with Kennedy. This theory hypothesizes that the Soviet Chairman intended to use the missile base as an effective bargaining power in a confrontation with the President to secure a favorable settlement on Berlin or to secure the withdrawal of U.S. overseas bases.[7]

According to the fifth theory, the Soviet Union sought to close the missile gap that favored the United States by emplacing missiles in Cuba so as to alter the strategic balance of missile power. Hence, by providing Cuban bases for their existing MRBMs and IRBMs, the Soviets sought a swift and relatively inexpensive means of adding to the total number of missiles targeted on the United States.[8]

Sorensen tends to accept the last theory with modification. The Cuban missiles alone did not substantially alter the strategic balance in actuality, but "that balance would have been

substantially altered in appearance . . . [and] such appear-
ances contribute to reality."[9] Nonetheless, whatever theory is
correct, it is evident that the Soviet missiles in Cuba did materially and politically change the balance of power in the Cold
War.[10]

With the missiles in Cuba effecting a change in the balance
of power in the Cold War, the members of Ex Com together
with the President decided that the situation necessitated a U.S.
response. According to Sorensen, Ex Com initially considered
six alternative courses of action: (1) do nothing, (2) bring diplomatic pressure via the United Nations or the Organization of
American States to bear upon the Soviet Union, (3) undertake
a secret approach to Castro in order to separate him from the
Soviets, (4) initiate indirect military action via a blockade, (5)
conduct an air strike on the missiles in Cuba, and (6) launch
an invasion of Cuba.[11] After numerous frustrations and dis-
agreements and after President Kennedy rejected the diplomatic alternative because the Soviet missiles in Cuba represented a deliberate deception and a provocative change in the
delicate status quo, the alternatives were reduced to either an
air strike or a blockade.[12]

Sorensen was against the air strike because it could not be
purely surgical; there also was no guarantee that all the missiles could be destroyed in a few sorties. Furthermore, the
problem of advance warning was unsolvable. An attack without warning would not be understood by the world, but any
warning of an air strike against Cuba would give Khrushchev
time to outmaneuver this form of U.S. action. Finally, any type
of air strike would likely kill some Russian technical personnel
in Cuba, which, in turn, would provoke a Soviet military response.[13]

Sorensen supported the blockade, later officially described as
a quarantine, because it was a limited, low-key form of military
action. The blockade had the advantage of "permitting a more
controlled escalation on our part, gradual or rapid as the situation required."[14] Sorensen also favored the blockade because
it could serve "as an unmistakable but not sudden or humiliating warning to Khrushchev of what we expected from him."[15]

In essence, Sorensen urged the President to accept the blockade because it was flexible, less aggressive than an air strike, less likely to precipitate war, and least likely of all the alternatives to cause the Soviets to escalate the confrontation.[16]

Why did the Soviets respect the quarantine of the United States? The President, according to Sorensen, believed that the Soviet Union was reluctant to have the United States halt Soviet ships on the high seas because of their highly secret and sensitive materials and because the Soviets could not risk the possibility of having their missiles and electronic equipment confiscated by their nuclear opponent.[17] Thus the quarantine underlined the value of conventional military strength in the nuclear age as a "minimum of force had obtained a maximum gain."[18]

Sorensen claims that the Cuban missile crisis was President Kennedy's finest hour. While the President was never lonelier than during the confrontation, he was neither hasty nor hesitant; he was neither reckless nor afraid. He "never lost sight of what either war or surrender would do to the whole human race . . . [and] he was determined to take all necessary action and no unnecessary action."[19] This is part of what Sorensen calls the Kennedy legacy: "a pervasive sense of responsibility for the future of our children . . . for those who live in this country and those who live in other lands."[20]

Sorensen contends that the result of the Cuban missile crisis was a reappraisal of communist policy. "He [Khrushchev] had looked down the gun barrel of nuclear war and decided that that course was suicidal."[21] The Soviet Chairman had tried nuclear blackmail and had failed; he had tested U.S. resolve and had found it determined. He had tried to gain nuclear superiority swiftly and had failed; he also had tested the U.S. President and had found him to be strong. As a result, the crisis removed conflict with the West from the top of the Soviet Union's agenda.[22]

Peaceful coexistence superseded conflict, and, for Sorensen, the value of peaceful coexistence became part of the Soviet Union's foreign policy. This new policy ultimately led to the installation of the teletype hot line between Washington and

Moscow and to the ratification of the Nuclear Test Ban Treaty, an accomplishment that brought President Kennedy his greatest satisfaction in the White House.[23]

Robert F. Kennedy's *Thirteen Days* (1969) is a short but intriguing presentation of the personalities and attitudes of those involved in the deliberations of Ex Com during the crisis days of October 1962.[24] The former Attorney General, who was a member of Ex Com, describes with intimacy the decision-making process of the President and his closest advisers during the height of the Cuban missile crisis.

While Secretary of Defense Robert S. McNamara was the first to propose a blockade as the initial response of the United States to the Soviet emplacement of missiles in Cuba, such action found its strongest supporter in the Attorney General, who argued that the blockade was the most flexible of any of the responses under consideration and that it was the only moral response available to the United States in terms of U.S. tradition. He denounced the option of an air attack because the bombing would kill civilians, and he denounced the option of an invasion because U.S. tradition would not permit such a course of action.[25] The most powerful argument against an air strike or an invasion was contained in a note from Robert Kennedy to the President: "I know how Tojo [Japanese Premier in 1941] felt when he was planning Pearl Harbor."[26] President Kennedy was not going to be America's Tojo.

According to memoirist Kennedy, the deliberations of Ex Com were conducted among equals as the President was often absent intentionally from the meetings. Therefore, there was no specific protocol; there was no place for rank. Undersecretaries often challenged and disagreed with their superiors. The group did not even have an official chairman. The discussions "were completely uninhibited and unrestricted."[27] Politics generally were kept to a minimum. Yet, after the announcement of the quarantine, Robert Kennedy admits that in a conversation with the President he stated: "If you hadn't acted, you would have been impeached."[28] The presidential agreement to this statement indicated that the crisis was not entirely without its political implications.

According to U.S. calculations, neither the United States nor the Soviet Union wanted war. Yet it was possible that either the Americans or the Soviets could miscalculate. Either of the two nuclear powers could take a position that would bring a counterresponse and eventually an escalation into armed conflict. This is what the President wanted to avoid. "He did not want anyone to be able to say that the U.S. had not done all it could to preserve the peace."[29]

One of the most perplexing issues of the Cuban crisis revolves around the U.S. Jupiter missiles in Turkey. Only Robert Kennedy could have clarified the issue but he failed to do so. The point in question is whether the Attorney General officially promised Soviet Ambassador Dobrynin in their meeting of Saturday evening, October 27, that the United States would withdraw its missiles from Turkey if the Soviet Union would terminate the nuclear confrontation by withdrawing its missiles from Cuba. At the Kennedy-Dobrynin meeting, the Soviet Ambassador to the United States raised the question about the U.S. missiles in Turkey. Kennedy replied that there could be no quid pro quo, but he also explained that within a short time after the resolution of the crisis the obsolete missiles in Turkey would be removed.[30] Was this an official or a personal pledge? Was it even considered a pledge or a concession in secret diplomacy? The Attorney General is vague on this point. Khrushchev, however, apparently considered it a diplomatic pledge, for, in his memoir, he contends that the Soviet Union decided to conclude the crisis on the basis of the U.S. promise to withdraw its missiles from Turkey and Italy.[31] Therefore, it appears that Kennedy did offer some type of concession, either officially or personally, and the Soviets did consider it an official diplomatic pledge.

According to the Attorney General, everyone was consumed with concern and trepidation during the crisis, but also everyone was filled "with a sense of pride in the strength, the purposefulness, and the courage of the President of the United States."[32] Like Sorensen, Robert Kennedy describes a President responding magnificently to the crisis situation. The President constantly placed himself in the position of Chairman Khrushchev. "Always he asked himself: Can we be sure that Khrushchev understands what we feel to be our vital interest?"[33] The President sought neither to affect Soviet national security nor to humiliate Khrushchev publicly. President Kennedy constantly was committed to do everything to lessen the chance of error, mistake, miscalculation, and misunderstanding.[34]

In "The Presidency and the Peace," an article that appeared in *Foreign Affairs* in 1964, McGeorge Bundy, Special Assistant to the President for National Security Affairs and a member of Ex Com, praises President Kennedy for his responsible use of power and for his personal management of the nuclear confrontation.[35] In the same vein as Ted Sorensen and Bob Kennedy, Bundy lists the components of presidential success in the missile crisis as "strength, restraint, and respect for the opinions of mankind."[36] Despite the President's youth, grace, and wit, the essential leadership qualities exhibited by Kennedy in the crisis were his courage, vision, resolution, and humanity; it was these qualities, combined with an acute sense of responsibility, that governed the United States in the days of October 1962.[37]

The basic thesis of the Bundy article is that "the armed strength of the United States, if handled with firmness and prudence, is a great force for peace."[38] Bundy implies but never states explicitly that it was the combined conventional and nuclear military strength of the United States and the President's willingness to risk nuclear war that effected a peaceful resolution of the missile crisis. Thus, the interpretation of Bundy, a hawk in the crisis deliberations, counters the implications of Sorensen and Kennedy who were doves. According to Sorensen, had the quarantine failed, the President "would not have moved immediately to either an air strike or an invasion."[39] Therefore, by implication, Sorensen suggests that President Kennedy was hesitant about provoking a possible nuclear response; he did not feel free to risk a nuclear war.

Swords and Plowshares (1972) is a record of the recollections of General Maxwell D. Taylor, Chairman of the Joint Chiefs of Staff and a participant in the Ex Com meetings during the Cuban missile crisis.[40] Like Bundy, General Taylor was a hawk; he was one from start to finish, "first as the spokesman for the Joint Chiefs of Staff, then from personal conviction."[41]

Commenting on possible Soviet motives, Taylor lists five plausible reasons for the Soviets emplacing missiles in Cuba: (1) to defend Cuba from U.S. invasion, (2) to increase with a minimum of Soviet financial expenditures the coverage of U.S. targets by strategic nuclear weapons, (3) to bargain the removal of Soviet missiles in Cuba for the removal of U.S. missiles in Turkey and Italy, (4) to divert the United States from the defense of Berlin, and (5) to strengthen Khrushchev's leadership in the Soviet Politburo.[42] Of these five motives, Taylor tends to give primary credence to the fifth as being most consistent with the Soviet effort to deceive Kennedy about Soviet intentions in Cuba as the Russians simultaneously and secretly introduced nuclear warheads on the island.[43]

Why did U.S. intelligence fail to detect the missiles until mid-October? According to Taylor, the perceptivity of U.S. intelligence was dulled by the profusion of implausible rumors and by the confusion of reports from Cubans as to the differentiating factor between defensive and offensive weapons. U.S. intelligence also could not imagine Khrushchev entrusting nuclear missiles to Castro, especially in view of the fact that the Soviets had never permitted the installation of Soviet nuclear bases outside the frontiers of Russia.[44] Thus, Taylor's reaction on learning of the critical situation in Cuba was "primarily one of incredulous amazement."[45] He simply could not comprehend Khrushchev being so foolhardly as to challenge the United States in a geographical location where he was at such "a tremendous political and military disadvantage."[46]

Taylor was the strongest supporter of an air strike among Ex Com members. The reasons for the general's support of an air strike were based on the following assumptions: (1) the missiles could become operational within a few days; (2) the Cubans were unaware of the U.S. discovery and, therefore, the missile sites enjoyed only limited protection from the Cuban air defense system; and (3) any delay might permit the Cubans to disperse the missiles into the forests where they could be destroyed successfully only by an invasion.[47] Taylor reasoned that an air strike followed by a complete blockade of Cuba and by preparation for an invasion of the island would induce Khrushchev to dismantle the missiles.[48]

The Chairman of the Joint Chiefs of Staff refused to accept the Attorney General's argument that an air strike had all the connotations of a Pearl Harbor with the United States cast "in the role of the perfidious aggressor."[49] According to Taylor, President Kennedy's previous explicit warnings of the dire consequences of Soviet offensive military bases in Cuba eliminated any analogy between Pearl Harbor and an air attack on Cuba. Moreover, General Taylor believed that the quarantine was much more likely to develop into a choice "between invading Cuba or backing down than was the seemingly more violent alternative of the air attack."[50] And, for Taylor, invading Cuba was something the United States could not afford to do militarily or politically.[51]

Against charges that the military seeks violent solutions to international problems, General Taylor emphasizes that the Joint Chiefs, as a group, never recommended an invasion, and it was Lieutenant General Sweeney of the Tactical Air Command who tipped the scale in favor of the quarantine over the air attack by conceding that an attack could not guarantee the destruction or neutralization of all the nuclear missiles on the island.[52] Yet, in the end, the crisis was not terminated by diplomatic persuasion but by "the growing impatience of the President backed by his formidable invasion force ready to strike."[53]

How responsible was President Kennedy in the crisis? While Khrushchev was caught by surprise and displayed symptoms of shock, the U.S. President seized the initiative and proceeded calmly to execute a thoroughly devised plan of action. Taylor claims that President Kennedy behaved as responsibly as any world leader could have behaved under the circumstances; he sought minimum risks while acting immediately and decisively to avoid a dangerously prolonged confrontation.[54] The approach Kennedy took was cautious, but at the same time it was a classic example of "the use of military power for political purposes which is the prime justification for military power."[55]

As time elapses, confrontations tend to appear less frightening and less deterministic than at the moment of their occurrences. This appears to be true with the Cuban missile crisis. Hence, Sorensen, Kennedy, and Bundy, writing in the 1960s, give the impression that nuclear war was a real possibility, but

Taylor, writing in the 1970s, claims that he was "never particularly afraid of either side using nuclear weapons unless through some hideous miscalculation."[56]

Arthur M. Schlesinger, Jr., former Special Assistant to the President and a member of the U.S. delegation to the United Nations during the Cuban missile crisis, has written two books that describe, in part, the nuclear crisis of October 1962. The first of these books is a portrait of President Kennedy entitled *A Thousand Days* (1965).[57] The second is a portrait of Attorney General Kennedy and is entitled *Robert Kennedy and His Times* (1978).[58]

U.S. intelligence grossly miscalculated Soviet intentions in Cuba in the summer and fall of 1962, according to Schlesinger. U.S. intelligence experts on Soviet foreign policy could not imagine the Soviet Union going beyond the emplacement of defensive weapons in a communist satellite country; the experts considered Russian policy too rational for such a risk. Schlesinger believes that intelligence experts in Russia must have known that offensive missiles in Cuba would legitimatize a U.S. response. Chairman Khrushchev apparently considered the risk worthwhile in an attempt to destroy world trust in U.S. resolve.[59] Nonetheless, the attempt was a staggering project: "staggering in its recklessness, staggering in its misconception of the American response, staggering in its rejection of the ground rules for coexistence among the superpowers. . . ."[60]

Schlesinger disclaims the theory that the Soviets put nuclear missiles in Cuba solely for defensive purposes; rather, he concentrates on a host of international and domestic problems facing Russia in 1962. In foreign affairs, Khrushchev was blocked in his design to take over Berlin, challenged by Peking for world leadership of communism, and stalled in his efforts to advance communism in the Third World. In domestic affairs, Khrushchev was challenged by the Soviet generals for a larger share of the limited financial resources for the military budget and by the Stalinists for a reduction in internal liberalization. Finally, Khrushchev was under pressure to redress the inordinate imbalance in strategic nuclear power between the United States and the Soviet Union.[61] Thus, with one roll of the nuclear dice, Khrushchev sought to "redress the strategic imbalance, humiliate the Americans, rescue the Cubans, silence the Stalinists and the generals, confound the Chinese and acquire a potent bargaining counter when he chose to replay Berlin."[62]

According to Schlesinger, Khrushchev believed that the emplacement of offensive nuclear weapons in Cuba would be a victory of the highest significance for the Soviet Union, for it would demonstrate to the world that the Russians could act with impunity in an area of U.S. vital interest. Khrushchev, of course, assumed that once the nuclear missiles were operational, Kennedy, being a rational man, would not initiate a nuclear war in order to remove them.[63]

Schlesinger believes that President Kennedy had no other option than to seek the removal of the missiles. The offensive nuclear weapons represented an unjustified and a deliberatively provocative change in the balance of power.[64]

To do nothing, simply to acquiesce, "would have been a stunning vindication of the Soviet 'Cold War of movement' . . . [and] would have produced a shattering reaction in the United States."[65]

Against charges that the President exploited the crisis for political reasons, Schlesinger contends that the quarantine was a nonpolitical measure. If the President had wished to exploit the crisis, he would have implemented an air strike as advocated by the Republicans. This was the one course of action "that would infallibly have insured a Democratic triumph in 1962. . . ."[66]

Schlesinger claims that the President's policy of giving Khrushchev and the Kremlin time to think prevented the crisis from developing into nuclear war. After the quarantine was established, the President made three vital decisions that promoted the cause of a peaceful solution. The first vital decision was to prevent any unnecessary incident on the high seas. The second vital decision was to refuse U.N. Secretary-General U Thant's proposal that the United States suspend the quarantine in exchange for the Soviet Union's suspension of its arms shipments to Cuba while simultaneously authorizing U.S. Ambassador Adlai Stevenson to continue discussions at the United Nations on whether a satisfactory arrangement could be effected for the removal of the missiles. The third vital decision was to permit a Soviet tanker, the *Bucharest*, to proceed through the quarantine on October 25 without boarding and searching it. These decisions, then, provided the basis for the turning point in the crisis of nuclear confrontation.[67]

Schlesinger theorizes that Khrushchev knew early in the crisis that his gamble had failed. The Soviet Chairman knew that any attempt to take over Berlin would expose the Soviet Union to nuclear attack by the United States. He also knew that not to effect a change in the Cuban situation would invite U.S. invasion of the Caribbean island.[68]

Schlesinger attributes "accidents of history" as reinforcing Khrushchev's determination to terminate the crisis. He cites the unauthorized statement of Lincoln White, a press officer in the State Department, suggesting on October 26 that "further action" may be necessary. He also cites the U-2 flight of October 27 that accidentally strayed from its course and flew over the Soviet Union as perhaps being interpreted in the Kremlin as a reconnaissance flight preceding a U.S. attack. These two incidents combined with the Soviet knowledge of the presence of an invasion force in Florida may well have influenced Khrushchev to seek an end to the confrontation.[69]

Another reason why Khrushchev may have sought a termination of the crisis, according to Schlesinger, is that "the Kennedys made a personal, but not an official, pledge that the Turkish missiles would go."[70] Thus, Schlesinger suggests that this additional concession on the part of the United States "doubtless helped persuade the Russians that the American government was truly bent on peace."[71] Schlesinger, therefore, claims that President Kennedy did not reject diplomacy in favor of confrontation, but rather he followed the diplomatic path in the Kennedy-Dobrynin talks after arranging a military setting that insured the success of diplomacy.[72]

According to Schlesinger, after the resolution of the crisis, President Kennedy feared that the American people might believe wrongly that a firm policy automatically would cause the Soviet Union to collapse in any confrontation. However, he warned the author that there were three distinct features of the Cuban crisis. Had these features not been present, events may not have occurred as they did. The Cuban crisis took place in a geographical area where the United States enjoyed conventional military superiority. The crisis occurred in a situation in which Soviet national security was not directly threatened, and it took place under circumstances in which the Soviet Union lacked a legitimate case to present to the world.[73]

Schlesinger claims that President Kennedy responded superbly to the crisis with toughness, restraint, determination, and wisdom. He measured every level of response objectively and precisely to the level of threat. Thus, the ultimate impact of the crisis was to display to the world "the ripening of an American leadership unsurpassed in the responsible management of power."[74] The days of the October crisis showed U.S. determination in the responsible use of power, which "might indeed become a turning point in the history of relations between east and west."[75]

The missile crisis was a triumph, a triumph of flexible response, according to Schlesinger.[76] Furthermore, if the missile crisis had not been resolved, there would have been no hot line and no test ban treaty; the détente symbolized by these items brought relief from the intolerable pressures of the Cold War. Most importantly, the successful resolution of the Cuban missile crisis made détente not only possible but imperative.[77]

Schlesinger admits that at the time of the crisis the possibility of war seemed high, not because of Khrushchev's intentions but because of the possibility of human error. Although the Kennedys and McNamara did not relish a crisis, most of the New Frontiersmen liked the challenge of a confrontation, which may have added to the tumult of emotion. In retrospect, however, Schlesinger believes that the risk of war, estimated at the time to be one in three or even, was exaggerated.[78] Yet, even assuming rationality on the part of the Americans and the Soviets, "a terrible risk remained."[79]

"The Cuban missile crisis was a dazzling success. And so, most importantly, was the follow-up—the nuclear test ban treaty and the measured steps toward a détente. . . . "[80] This is the view held by Roger Hilsman in his *To Move a Nation* (1967). This book is an analytical account by the former Director of Intelligence and Research for the State Department in the Kennedy era.

The Soviet emplacement of missiles in Cuba was a strategic response to Russian military, economic, and political problems. The Soviet Union's policy was motivated by a desire to project Russian influence in the Western Hemisphere and to extend communism. If missiles were emplaced successfully in Cuba, Russia would emerge as the leader in world communism. Such a success not only would provide Russia with leverage on Berlin, but also it would counter the domestic problems in the Soviet economy.[81]

According to Hilsman, American intelligence firmly believed that Soviet foreign policy was too cautious for the Russians to install offensive missiles in Cuba, especially since the Soviets had not even permitted offensive missiles in Eastern Europe. Furthermore, U.S. intelligence reasoned that the likelihood of discovery was so high as to make such action improbable. Finally, Castro himself was unstable and thus most unlikely to be a recipient of offensive missiles.[82]

As Hilsman suggests, the first and ultimately the most serious error that the Soviets made was their miscalculation of the probable U.S. response. The Soviet Union assumed that either the United States would protest and then finally acquiesce or the United States would threaten and then negotiate, perhaps on Turkey or Berlin. It was a gamble that the Soviet Union considered worth the minimum risk.[83]

The United States could permit a gradual change in the strategic balance of power, but it could not tolerate a sudden change such as that represented by offensive missiles in Cuba.[84] Thus Kennedy had to respond to this crisis. He was determined not to be dragged along by events but to control them.[85] The blockade permitted such a response, for it "permitted a step by step progression up the ladder of coercion. . . ."[86]

Why did the Soviet Union back down in Cuba? According to Hilsman, the Soviet leaders probably were confident that whatever the U.S. response, such would begin with conventional weapons. The Soviets apparently believed that unless they did something completely unconventional, the United States would confine itself to conventional warfare. However, they also must have been aware that any limited war can escalate to nuclear war. Thus the Soviet leadership backed down because of a U.S.

threat that combined both conventional and nuclear power. It was a threat of on-the-spot conventional superiority and overall nuclear superiority.[87]

The emplacement of Soviet missiles in Cuba clearly was threatening to the United States and irresponsible on the part of the Soviet leadership. Yet the withdrawal of the missiles by the Soviets required courage which they displayed. The crisis also revealed the wisdom and restraint that could be exercised by the Soviet leadership.[88]

Hilsman contends that President Kennedy made no strategic mistakes in his crisis response and diplomacy. He exercised wisdom, analysis, and a keen sense of strategy. Kennedy's leadership during the Cuban missile crisis illustrated that he "understood that the true art of statecraft is not always to adjust to events or always to attempt to dictate them, but to distinguish between those to which we must adjust and those which we may influence."[89] To Hilsman, John F. Kennedy was not only a leader but also a hero.[90]

The Diffusion of Power (1972) is another memoir by a key figure in the Kennedy administration.[91] Written by Walt W. Rostow, Chairman of the Policy Planning Council of the State Department during the missile crisis, the book is a study of U.S. domestic and foreign policies between 1958 and 1972 with special emphasis on the diffusion of power in the world arena.

According to Rostow, Khrushchev needed some kind of successful incident to raise his shrinking prestige by the spring of 1962; everywhere he was being held at bay. Khrushchev had committed himself on the Berlin issue but was unable to shift the Western position. He had failed to expand successfully in the Congo and in Southeast Asia. Also, Castro had become neutralized by the Organization of American States; as in Southeast Asia, the prospects for communist expansion in Latin America were dim.[92] Thus, by the spring of 1962,

Khrushchev was looking for a quick success which would enhance his political prestige and power in Soviet politics; enhance his authority in the international communist movement . . . redress the military balance cheaply in terms of resources . . . and provide leverage for the resolution of the Berlin problem he had sought without success since 1958.[93]

Rostow believes that the Soviet plan for the emplacement of missiles in Cuba was primarily Khrushchev's brainchild. While the Presidium acquiesced, it was Khrushchev's political career that was at stake.[94]

While Khrushchev knew President Kennedy's position on the balance of power and on the Monroe Doctrine, and while he understood the OAS posture on foreign military intrusion in Latin America, Rostow still contends that the installation of missiles in Cuba must have seemed to Khrushchev to have been legal according to international law, "as legal as the placing of American missiles in Turkey."[95] Hence, Khrushchev believed he had assessed accurately the situation and was willing to gamble for the sake of prestige. "What he did not assess correctly is the depth of feeling and determination his act would evoke from Kennedy . . . and the unanimity of the hemispheric response."[96]

In harmony with other officials of the Kennedy administration, Rostow praises the President's personal command of the crisis and his choice of a blockade. The genius of the blockade was "that it required Khrushchev to initiate military action."[97]

Rostow discusses two major effects that resulted from the Cuban crisis. First, the crisis eroded Khrushchev's power base in Moscow; second, it led to a violent and open controversy between Moscow and Peking.[98] Therefore, the ultimate result of the crisis and the subsequent détente with the United States "served to accelerate the diffusion of power within the communist and noncommunist worlds."[99]

In *The Cuban Missile Crisis* (1974), Abram Chayes discusses the importance of international law in the nuclear confrontation of 1962.[100] The former Chief Legal Adviser in the State Department describes the role and the impact of law during the crisis and, especially, during the deliberations that resulted in the implementation of the U.S. quarantine of Cuba.

According to Chayes, international law acted as a constraint on the choice of the quarantine. Law also served as a justification for the quarantine by reference to the Organization of American States, as it provided the organizational structure for action under the United Nations. Initially, international law restrained the action of the United States because Article Two of the U.N. Charter ruled out the use of land aggression and surprise air attack. Thus, Article Two significantly affected the decision of the United States to use a quarantine.[101]

The United States sought public justification in its decision to use the quarantine. This justification was sought through reference of the decision to the OAS. The United States knew that "approval by that body would immeasurably strengthen the justification" of its action because then the United States would be acting in concert with others in an international organization.[102] Such collective action is considered more balanced and less biased in world affairs than unilateral action.[103] Hence, legal justification "influenced not only the execution but the choice of quarantine as well."[104]

The United Nations provided the organizational structure, procedure, and forum for the discussion and resolution of the legal issue. The United Nations provided the two conflicting nuclear powers with a common place to influence world opinion, which is vitally important in international law. The United Nations also provided the United States with an organization for generating support for and neutralizing opposition to its program of action in the international crisis.[105]

Those who were responsible for decisions during the crisis did not fail to consider the legal ramifications. Considerable effort was made to integrate legal factors into the deliberations. Evidence of this is to be found in the three briefs of the departments of State, Defense, and Justice. "Law and legal institutions played a part in defining and shaping those possibilities" of U.S. reaction to the crisis.[106]

Johnny, We Hardly Knew Ye (1970) is a memoir focusing on the development of John F. Kennedy as a politician from his first race for Congress to his death.[107] Written primarily by Kenneth P. O'Donnell, Appointments Secretary to President Kennedy, with insights from David F. Powers, personal confidant of the President, the book is a mass of comic and trivial detail. Yet the authors do have their serious side, such as when they explain the Cuban missile crisis.

O'Donnell believes that the Soviets introduced missiles into Cuba for their own defense rather than for the defense of the Caribbean island. Basing his hypothesis on the papers of Col onel Oleg Penkovskiy, an Allied spy in Russia, O'Donnell claims that Russia in 1962 did not possess many long-range intercontinental ballistic missiles; most of the ICBMs were either on the drawing boards or in the prototype testing stage. Chairman Khrushchev therefore took the risk of putting operational short-range missiles into Cuba to defend the Soviet Union from U.S. attack in case of a nuclear war.[108]

President Kennedy never believed that the missiles in Cuba truly changed the balance of military power, according to O'Donnell. He did, however, consider it a direct thrust at U.S. credibility and believed that to acquiesce in the Soviet intrusion into the Western Hemisphere would have been "a tremendous psychological blow."[109] Therefore, President Kennedy decided to outmaneuver Khrushchev by secretly ruling out a diplomatic or a political approach and clandestinely planning a quarantine.[110]

O'Donnell praises President Kennedy's statesmanship during the U.S.-Soviet confrontation. The President was calm and relaxed during the whole hectic episode.[111] He appeared as "a rock of solid good sense and unwavering strength and firmness."[112] O'Donnell even attributes the break in the alliance between Russia and China to "President Kennedy's firm and successful stand against Khrushchev during the Cuban missile crisis."[113]

Pierre Salinger, Press Secretary to the President, was not informed of the crisis until Sunday, October 21, one day before President Kennedy's address to the nation. Hence, Salinger's *With Kennedy* (1966) adds very little to the literature of the Cuban missile crisis.[114] Nonetheless, Salinger's story is informative in that it explains how the government handles its news in a national security situation.

Salinger relates numerous incidents that caused press credibility problems during the crisis. These incidents included: (1) Salinger's informing the press in Chicago on October 20 that the President had to return to Washington because of a cold, an incident for which Salinger was accused of lying to the press although he had not as of that date been informed of the crisis; (2) Congressman James Van Zandt's announcement, following a congressional briefing, that the Soviet tanker *Bucharest* had been intercepted, searched, and allowed to proceed through the quarantine line before the official news was released by the Department of Defense; (3) the release of the photographic intelligence showing the nuclear missiles in Cuba by Ambassador Bruce to the British press before such pictures were made available to the U.S. press; and (4) the governmental request for voluntary censorship of certain categories of information by news directors throughout the country, which some saw fit to follow while others did not.[115] The result of these incidents led to media associations condemning the Kennedy administration for "generation of news" and for "management of the news."[116]

Salinger defends the government's handling of the news during the crisis and his own part therein by claiming that national security required government generation of the news. According to the Press Secretary, the question is "how a democracy . . . defends itself in a cold-war situation against an enemy which can operate in secret."[117]

Like all the previous authors from the Kennedy administration, Salinger leaves no doubt as to the magnificent leadership the President exhibited during the grimmest days of his administration. The Press Secretary states unequivocally: "I never knew him [the President] to be more in command of himself or of events. And I can never forget his courage, his smile, and his optimism."[118]

The traditionalists, writing from the perspective of former personnel in the Kennedy administration, do reach consensus in numerous areas. Several of the administrators agree on the initial miscalculations of intelligence agencies. Soviet intelligence seriously miscalculated the determined U.S. response (Sorensen, Schlesinger, Rostow) and assumed that the United States would either protest and acquiesce or threaten and negotiate (Hilsman). The Soviets also miscalculated the solidarity of Western hemispheric unity in the crisis (Rostow).

U.S. intelligence equally was vulnerable to miscalculation. U.S. intelligence considered the Soviet Union too cautious and restrained to put missiles in unstable Castro's Cuba where discovery was all too likely (Hilsman) and where the United States enjoyed a tremendous military advantage (Taylor). U.S. intelligence experts considered Soviet foreign and military policies too rational to emplace offensive weapons in Cuba where such action would legitimatize a U.S. response (Schlesinger).

Conceding that the Soviets miscalculated the response of the United States to the emplacement of ballistic missiles in Cuba, what motives originally generated the grand design? While the true Russian motives may never be known, several possible theories have been advanced. Among the most prevalent hypotheses are: (1) the Soviets sought to test U.S. national determination and/or Kennedy's will and determination (Sorensen, Schlesinger); (2) the Russians sought to strengthen their bargaining position on Berlin (Sorensen, Taylor, Schlesinger, Hilsman, Rostow); (3) Khrushchev and his associates sought to defend Cuba from a U.S. attack while simultaneously extending the communist influence in the Western Hemisphere (Sorensen, Taylor, Schlesinger, Hilsman, O'Donnell); (4) the Soviets sought to alter and equalize the strategic balance of power (Sorensen, Taylor, Schlesinger, Hilsman, Rostow); (5) Khrushchev and/or the Russians sought to reassert their authority and prestige as the leader in international communism (Sorensen, Taylor, Hilsman, Rostow); and (6) Khrushchev sought to divert attention away from a host of Soviet domestic problems (Schlesinger, Hilsman).

While the traditionalists disagree over the question of whether the missiles affected the military, political, or psychological balance of power, they are all in agreement, either explicitly or implicitly, that the emplacement of Soviet offensive nuclear missiles in Cuba did alter, either literally or in appearance, the status quo of the balance of power, especially in an area of vital interest to the United States (Sorensen, Kennedy, Bundy, Taylor, Schlesinger, Hilsman, Rostow, Chayes, O'Donnell, Salinger). Therefore, President Kennedy had no other option than to act.

While Taylor and Bundy advocated an air strike, the consensus of Ex Com supported a quarantine, for such action provided a flexible, step-by-step progression on the ladder of coercion (Sorensen, Kennedy, Schlesinger, Hilsman) and required Khrushchev to be the first to initiate military action (Rostow). Equally as important, however, was the fact that it was normally more acceptable than an air strike or an invasion (Sorensen, Kennedy); there was also a basis in international law to support the quarantine (Chayes). Finally, except for Taylor and Bundy, the traditionalists contend, either implicitly or explicitly, that the quarantine exerted maximum pressure for the minimum risks involved.

The participants in the crisis within the Kennedy administration generally assume that the Soviet Union agreed to withdraw the missiles because of the implicit threat posed by the U.S. conventional military superiority in this hemisphere and overall nuclear superiority (Sorensen, Bundy, Taylor, Schlesinger, Hilsman). However, others add, implicitly or explicitly, that the diplomatic path of pledging to withdraw U.S. missiles in Turkey hastened the Soviet decision to terminate the crisis (Kennedy, Schlesinger).

For the officials in the Kennedy administration, the Cuban missile crisis represented the President's finest hour. Kennedy was always in command of himself and of the crisis (Rostow, Salinger); he was neither reckless nor afraid, neither hasty nor hesitant (Sorensen). The President acted cautiously and responsibly (Taylor) with courage, vision, firmness, good sense, and unwavering strength (Bundy, O'Donnell). He controlled events rather than being controlled by them, and he judged accurately that to which he had to adjust and that which he could influence (Hilsman). The President gave Khrushchev time to respond to U.S. action, which neither affected Soviet national security nor humiliated Khrushchev (Kennedy). In the final analysis, the President measured every level of response objectively and precisely, and in doing so he exhibited unsurpassed qualities in the responsible management of power (Schlesinger). By showing Chairman Khrushchev the edge of the nuclear abyss, President Kennedy's leadership in the crisis led to a reduction in the tensions of the Cold War and to the installation of a hot line as well as to the signing of a nuclear test ban treaty; the crisis thus helped to promote peaceful co-existence and détente between the United States and the Soviet Union (Sorensen, Schlesinger, Hilsman, Rostow).

NOTES

1. Theodore C. Sorensen, *Kennedy* (New York: Harper and Row, 1965; paperback ed., New York: Bantam Books, 1966). See also by the same author, *Decision Making in the White House: The Olive Branch or the Arrows* (New York: Columbia University Press, 1963) and *The Kennedy Legacy* (New York: Macmillan, 1969). On March 5, 1987, Sorensen and seven other former members of the Kennedy administration met in Florida to discuss their perspectives of the crisis from the vantage point of twenty-five years of hindsight. For a description of these proceedings, see J. Anthony Lukas, "Class Reunion: Kennedy's Men Relive the Cuban Missile Crisis," *New York Times Magazine*, August 30, 1987; pp. 22–27 ff.

2. Sorensen, *Kennedy*, pp. 762–64.

3. *Ibid.*

4. *Ibid.*, pp. 862–63.

5. *Ibid.*, p. 763.

6. *Ibid.* According to Nikita Khrushchev and Anatolii Gromyko, the Soviets placed missiles in Cuba solely for the defense of the island republic. See Nikita S. Khrushchev, *Khrushchev Remembers*, trans. Strobe Talbott (Boston: Little, Brown, 1970), pp. 493–94. See also Anatolii A. Gromyko, *Through Russian Eyes: President Kennedy's 1036 Days* (Washington, D.C.: International Library, 1973), pp. 171–72.

7. Sorensen, *Kennedy*, pp. 763–64.

8. *Ibid.*, p. 764.

9. *Ibid.*

10. *Ibid.* For an analysis of the significance of the missiles, see Arnold L. Horelick, "The Cuban Missile Crisis: An Analysis of Soviet Calculations and Behavior," *World Politics* 16 (April 1964): 364–77. See also Jerome H. Kahan and Anne K. Long, "The Cuban Missile Crisis: A Study of Its Strategic Context," *Political Science Quarterly* 87 (December 1972): 564–90.

11. Sorensen, *Kennedy*, p. 769.

12. *Ibid.*, p. 771.

13. *Ibid.*, p. 771–73.

14. *Ibid.*, p. 776.

15. *Ibid.*

16. *Ibid.*, pp. 776–77, 782–83.

17. *Ibid.*, p. 801.

18. *Ibid.*

19. *Ibid.*, p. 795.

20. Sorensen, *Kennedy Legacy*, p. 274.

21. Sorensen, *Kennedy*, p. 815.

22. *Ibid.*, pp. 815–16.

23. *Ibid.*, p. 833.

24. Robert F. Kennedy, *Thirteen Days: A Memoir of the Cuban Missile Crisis* (New York: W. W. Norton, 1969).

25. *Ibid.*, pp. 37–38.

26. *Ibid.*, p. 31.

27. *Ibid.*, p. 46. For a contrary analysis of the Ex Com deliberations, see Dean Acheson, "Dean Acheson's Version of Robert Kennedy's Version of the Cuban Missile Affair: Homage to Plain Dumb Luck," *Esquire*, February 1969, pp. 44–46, 76–77.

28. Kennedy, *Thirteen Days*, p. 67.

29. *Ibid.*, p. 62.

30. *Ibid.*, pp. 108–09. The intermediate-range Jupiter missiles originally had been emplaced in Turkey during the Eisenhower administration as part of the NATO defense system. President Kennedy had ordered the removal of the missiles early in 1962 because he had considered them obsolete. The President, therefore, was surprised and angered to discover that the missiles were still in Turkey at the time of the missile crisis and that they were a liability as Khrushchev sought to use them in his negotiations to terminate the crisis. See James A. Nathan, "The Missile Crisis: His Finest Hour Now," *World Politics* 27 (January 1975): 267–71; Donald L. Hafner, "Bureaucratic Politics and 'Those Frigging Missiles': JFK, Cuba and U.S. Missiles in Turkey," *Orbis* 21 (Summer 1977): 307–33; Robert L. Perry, *The Ballistic Missile Decisions* (Santa Monica, Calif.: RAND Corporation, 1967), p. 22.

31. Nikita S. Khrushchev, *Khrushchev Remembers: The Last Testament*, trans. Strobe Talbott (Boston: Little, Brown, 1974), p. 512.

32. Kennedy, *Thirteen Days*, p. 56.

33. *Ibid.*, p. 125.

34. *Ibid.*, p. 127.

35. McGeorge Bundy, "The Presidency and the Peace," *Foreign Affairs* 42 (April 1964): 353–65.

36. *Ibid.*, 359.

37. *Ibid.*, 361–64.

38. *Ibid.*, 357.

39. Sorensen, *Kennedy*, p. 807.

40. Maxwell D. Taylor, *Swords and Plowshares* (New York: W. W. Norton, 1972).

41. *Ibid.*, p. 268.

42. *Ibid.*, pp. 277–78.

43. *Ibid.*, pp. 278–79.

44. *Ibid.*, p. 263.

45. *Ibid.*, p. 264.

46. *Ibid.*

47. *Ibid.*, p. 267.

48. *Ibid.*

49. *Ibid.*, p. 268.

50. *Ibid.*

51. *Ibid.*

52. *Ibid.*, pp. 269–71.

53. *Ibid.*, p. 277.

54. *Ibid.*, p. 279.

55. *Ibid.*, p. 280.

56. *Ibid.*, p. 268.

57. Arthur M. Schlesinger, Jr., *A Thousand Days: John F. Kennedy in the White House* (Boston: Houghton Mifflin, 1965; paperback ed., Greenwich, Conn.: Fawcett Publications, 1966).

58. Arthur M. Schlesinger, Jr., *Robert Kennedy and His Times* (Boston: Houghton Mifflin, 1978).

59. Schlesinger, *A Thousand Days*, pp. 729–30.

60. *Ibid.*, p. 729.

61. Schlesinger, *Robert Kennedy*, p. 504.

62. *Ibid.*

63. *Ibid.*

64. *Ibid.*, p. 506.

65. *Ibid.*, p. 512.

66. *Ibid.*, p. 517.

67. Schlesinger, *A Thousand Days*, pp. 749–51.

68. *Ibid.*, pp. 754–55.

69. *Ibid.*, p. 756.

70. Schlesinger, *Robert Kennedy*, p. 523.

71. *Ibid.*, p. 524.

72. *Ibid.*, p. 530.

73. Schlesinger, *A Thousand Days*, p. 759.

74. *Ibid.*, p. 767.

75. *Ibid.*, p. 769.

76. Schlesinger, *Robert Kennedy*, p. 528.

77. *Ibid.*, p. 530.

78. *Ibid.*, pp. 528–29.

79. *Ibid.*, p. 529.

80. Roger Hilsman, *To Move a Nation: The Politics of Foreign Policy in the Administration of John F. Kennedy* (Garden City, N.Y.: Doubleday,

1967), p. 581. See also by the same author, "The Cuban Missile Crisis: How Close We Were to War," *Look*, August 25, 1964, pp. 17–21.

81. Hilsman, *To Move a Nation*, pp. 161–64.

82. *Ibid.*, pp. 172–73. For a different perspective on the role and the problems of U.S. intelligence in discovering the missiles and in understanding Soviet behavior, see Roberta Wohlstetter, "Cuba and Pearl Harbor: Hindsight and Foresight," *Foreign Affairs* 43 (July 1965): 691–707. See also Klaus Knorr, "Failures in National Intelligence Estimates: The Case of the Cuban Missiles," *World Politics* 16 (April 1964): 455–67.

83. Hilsman, *To Move a Nation*, p. 186.

84. *Ibid.*, p. 202.

85. *Ibid.*, p. 198.

86. *Ibid.*, p. 205.

87. *Ibid.*, pp. 226–27.

88. *Ibid.*, p. 227.

89. *Ibid.*, p. 581.

90. *Ibid.*, p. 582.

91. Walt W. Rostow, *The Diffusion of Power: An Essay in Recent History* (New York: Macmillan, 1972). See also by the same author, *View from the Seventh Floor* (New York: Harper and Row, 1964).

92. Rostow, *Diffusion of Power*, p. 252.

93. *Ibid.*

94. *Ibid.*, p. 257.

95. *Ibid.*, p. 255.

96. *Ibid.*, p. 256.

97. *Ibid.*, p. 258.

98. *Ibid.*, p. 260.

99. *Ibid.*, p. 263.

100. Abram Chayes, *The Cuban Missile Crisis: International Crisis and the Role of Law* (New York: Oxford University Press, 1974). See also Leonard C. Meeker, "Defensive Quarantine and the Law," *American Journal of International Law* 57 (July 1963): 515–24; Charles G. Fenwick, "The Quarantine Against Cuba: Legal or Illegal?" *American Journal of International Law* 57 (July 1963): 588–92; Larman C. Wilson, "International Law and the United States Cuban Quarantine of 1962," *Journal of Inter-American Studies* 7 (October 1965): 485–92; Nicholas G. Onuf, "Law and Lawyers in International Crises," *International Organization* 29 (Autumn 1975): 1035–53.

101. Chayes, *Missile Crisis*, p. 40.

102. *Ibid.*, p. 68.

103. *Ibid.*, p. 50.

104. *Ibid.*, p. 68.

105. *Ibid.*, p. 49.

106. *Ibid.*, pp. 100–01.

107. Kenneth P. O'Donnell, David F. Powers, and Joe McCarthy, *Johnny, We Hardly Knew Ye: Memories of John Fitzgerald Kennedy* (Boston: Little, Brown, 1970).

108. *Ibid.*, p. 308. See Oleg Penkovskiy, *The Penkovskiy Papers*, trans. Peter Deriabin (Garden City, N.Y.: Doubleday, 1965).

109. O'Donnell et al., *Johnny*, p. 309.

110. *Ibid.*

111. *Ibid.*, p. 306.

112. *Ibid.*, p. 312.

113. *Ibid.*, p. 15.

114. Pierre Salinger, *With Kennedy* (Garden City, N.Y.: Doubleday, 1966).

115. *Ibid.*, pp. 286–94.

116. *Ibid.*, p. 296.

117. *Ibid.*, p. 299.

118. *Ibid.*, p. 267.

4

THE TRADITIONAL INTERPRETATION: THE OBSERVERS' PERSPECTIVE

The observer's perspective of the Cuban missile crisis in the traditional interpretive mode is fostered by two divergent groups, journalists and political scientists. The journalistic group is composed of correspondents who covered the confrontation as media assignments and who wrote their articles and books between 1962 and 1964. The political scientists, while not involved in the crisis in any way, began an analysis of the missile crisis soon after its termination, and their perspective continued to be published through the 1970s.

Despite the differences in their professional careers and the differences in the elapsed time between the crisis and their respective publications, the journalists and the political scientists present essentially the same perspective. Both believe that the successful resolution of the crisis represents President Kennedy's greatest achievement in the White House. Both conclude that the President successfully utilized nuclear brinkmanship and, therein, preserved the balance of power, world peace, and American values.

The traditional interpretation espoused by those writers outside the Kennedy administration follows the same general interpretive perspective as that fostered by the participants. There is, however, a slight shift in emphasis. The participants tend to emphasize the admirable qualities demonstrated by the President during the Cuban missile crisis while the observers tend to dwell on the President's ability to manage the crisis; that is, the latter stress the President's successful brinkmanship rather than his calmness and coolness during the confrontation.

In at least three major areas, the perspectives of the participants and the observers harmonize. First, in the area of intelligence, both agree that U.S. and Soviet intelligence experts grossly miscalculated each other's actions. Second, both agree that Chairman Khrushchev sought to change the status quo in the balance of power and that President Kennedy responded out of necessity to preserve that status quo and the credibility of U.S. defense commitments. Third, both participants and observers alike agree that President Kennedy responded to the crisis responsibly; his policy of combining caution with firmness led to the diffusion of the world's first nuclear confrontation.

Stewart Alsop and Charles Bartlett, both journalistic advocates of a firm U.S. foreign policy toward the Soviet Union, teamed together in December 1962 to compose the earliest version of the Cuban missile crisis by observers in the traditional interpretive mode. The article, "In Time of Crisis," appeared in the *Saturday Evening Post* and presented President Kennedy as a tough but flexible leader who stared at the Russians eyeball to eyeball until they blinked.[1]

As the first traditional interpretation of the nuclear confrontation of 1962, the article is noteworthy in many respects. It was the first piece of interpretive writing to identify the advocates of an air strike as hawks and the advocates of a blockade as doves. It was the first interpretation to praise Robert Kennedy for his advocacy of the blockade and for his suggestion to employ the "Trollope Ploy" in responding to the two contradictory letters of Chairman Khrushchev received on Friday night, October 26, and Saturday morning, October 27. Finally, it was the first article to suggest that Adlai Stevenson sought a "Munich" in his support of a proposition that the United States dismantle its bases in Turkey and Italy in exchange for Soviet bases in Cuba.[2]

According to Alsop and Bartlett, Khrushchev's objective in emplacing nuclear offensive missiles in Cuba was both strategic and political. If the missiles had become operative before their discovery, the early missile warning system of the United States would have been by-passed and "the whole strategic balance overturned."[3] Furthermore, operative missiles in Cuba would have rendered the United States "a paper tiger, a second-class power."[4] Such, then, would have overturned the political balance of power.

While cautioning against a belief that Khrushchev and the Soviet Union would always retreat in a nuclear confrontation, Alsop and Bartlett suggest that the crisis does indicate that if the United States responds firmly where its vital interests are threatened then the Soviets will "make all necessary [and] practical compromises. . . . "[5] Thus the pattern of the Cold War has been altered, because the crisis exposed Khrushchev and the Soviets as realists who, when communist doctrine conflicts with political reality, will be governed in their conduct by reality.[6]

Alsop and Bartlett conclude their article by enumerating the positive tangibles and intangibles that were made self-evident during the crisis. Among the positive tangibles were "the unanimous support of the Latin Americans, the staunchness of our European allies . . . [and] the exposure of Communist duplicity."[7] Among the positive intangibles were the inner sense of confidence of the members of Ex Com, who had near ultimate responsibility in the crisis, and the strength and unyielding nerve of the President, who carried the ultimate responsibility for the successful resolution of the confrontation.[8]

Hugh Sidey, journalist and political analyst for *Time* magazine, has written two accounts of President Kennedy in the Cuban missile crisis. The earliest account is primarily descriptive and appears in Sidey's full-length book, *John F. Kennedy, President* (1964).[9] The second account is analytical and was published originally in *Life* magazine in 1968 on the fifth anniversary of President Kennedy's assassination.[10]

In *John F. Kennedy, President*, Sidey reiterates the familiar traditional interpretation. Sidey contends that U.S. intelligence was lulled into a state of drowsiness by its intelligence experts who were convinced that the Russians would not permit Soviet offensive nuclear missiles outside the Soviet Union.[11] Why then did the Soviets emplace missiles in Cuba? According to Sidey,

Khrushchev gambled heavily "to tilt the balance of power in his favor, or at least to make it seem so to the world."[12]

Since President Kennedy believed that the missiles in Cuba represented an affront to the world balance of power, Sidey contends that Kennedy ordered a quarantine of Cuba, not as a measure to stop ships from bringing missiles to the Caribbean island, but as a "device to send the message of our determination through clearly to Nikita Khrushchev."[13] The quarantine put the prestige of the United States "on the line, backed with force."[14] This measure did not alienate U.S. allies in Latin America or in Europe, but it did give Khrushchev time to consider and to evaluate his own course of action.[15]

Sidey claims that the resolution of the missile crisis stands as President Kennedy's most enduring monument in that it represented "an understanding and use of the Presidency that has rarely been equaled in this nation's history."[16] The President moved cautiously through the crisis with time for thought and planning. From the outset, the President cast the missile crisis and the challenge it presented to the United States as "one of communication, not warfare."[17] In the final analysis, President Kennedy orchestrated the entire crisis from the perilous summit of passion down the long slope of "restraint and deliberation that led to the remarkable solution" to the nuclear missile crisis.[18]

As a result of the crisis, according to Sidey, the United States, as defender of the free world, "found itself held in rare esteem, and the stature of John Kennedy grew with it."[19] The President and the men of Ex Com "performed superbly in the thirteen critical days."[20]

William G. Carleton's article, "Kennedy in History: An Early Appraisal," originally published in *The Antioch Review* in 1964, is a balanced account of Kennedy as President.[21] While Professor Carleton is mildly critical of Kennedy, his interpretive perspective on the Cuban missile crisis places him within the traditional mode of interpretation for this event because, for Carleton, the U.S.-Soviet crisis of October 1962 represented "the high point, the turning point, in the Kennedy Administration."[22]

Carleton views President Kennedy's first two years in foreign policy as ambiguous, confused, and even contradictory. His analysis argues that Kennedy "fanned the tensions of the dying Cold War."[23] The President's inaugural address and his first State of the Union message were alarmist. His support of the Cuban invasion in April 1961 and his appeal to Americans to build bomb shelters produced a war psychology in the country.[24] It was not until the end of the second year and the beginning of the third year that Kennedy's foreign policy exhibited a sense of direction, "one which promised to harmonize American policy with emerging new realities in the world."[25]

According to Carleton, Khrushchev attempted to compensate for the U.S. intermediate-range ballistic missiles in Turkey and for his own lag in the construction of intercontinental missiles by secretly introducing offensive nuclear missiles in Cuba. Kennedy responded with the prudent use of force; the U.S. countermeasures, both military and diplomatic, were masterly. As a result of the crisis, Khrushchev and Castro lost prestige, but the United States won worldwide acclaim.[26]

The nuclear brinkmanship of the crisis, as Carleton claims, illustrated to the world "the lunacy of an ultimate nuclear showdown. . . ."[27] Thereafter, Khrushchev pursued a policy of peaceful coexistence, and Kennedy gave more recognition to the "common stake both the United States and the Soviet Union had in world peace and stability."[28] The new spirit in world affairs led to the first evidence of détente between the Americans and the Russians in the signing of a limited nuclear test ban treaty in the summer of 1963.[29] Hence, the nuclear crisis gave to President Kennedy a new awareness that the post-World War II period was ending; the crisis instilled in Kennedy a determination "to attempt more shifts in American foreign policy in harmony with the emerging fluidity."[30]

Richard E. Neustadt, professor of economics and political science at Harvard, wrote an essay in 1968 entitled "Afterword: JFK" which he included thereafter in his *Presidential Power*.[31] According to Neustadt, President Kennedy's greatest commitment during his tenure as President was "to reduce the risk of holocaust by mutual miscalculation, to get the nuclear genie back in the bottle."[32] This he successfully accomplished during and after the Cuban missile crisis. Thus the crisis permitted

President Kennedy to pioneer in the handling of nuclear confrontation; by his balancing of firmness with caution he dramatized what presidents must do to minimize the risk of nuclear destruction through mutual miscalculation. In his successful resolution of the world's first nuclear confrontation, President Kennedy "made a major contribution to the Presidency."[33]

In his essay, Neustadt assesses Kennedy's actions in the crisis from the perspectives of power and pressure. According to Neustadt, President Kennedy wisely exercised the power of his position in the U.S.-Soviet confrontation of 1962. While he took personal command of the situation, Kennedy did not seek victory; he displayed a concern for the psychology of Khrushchev and insisted on a limited objective—the removal of the offensive missiles in Cuba. Kennedy's operating power style and his control of the confrontation contributed to the successful termination of the crisis.[34]

How well did President Kennedy handle the pressures of the crisis? Remarkably well, contends Neustadt. The President was "cool, collected, courteous, and terse."[35] Despite the nerve-straining aspects of the crisis, Kennedy made decisions as a reasonable man. His confidence in himself under pressure matched his duty as President, and his reasonableness, despite the pressures of the confrontation, contributed to the successful conclusion of the crisis.[36]

Richard E. Neustadt expanded his analysis of the crisis in conjunction with Graham T. Allison in an "Afterword" to the 1971 edition of Robert F. Kennedy's *Thirteen Days*.[37] According to Neustadt, the Cuban missile crisis is important at three distinct levels. First, the crisis illustrated something central to our time: namely, man now controls the power to destroy all of mankind. Second, the crisis highlighted the dilemmas of decision making in a bureaucratic governmental system. Third, the crisis dramatized the role of the President in deciding the issue of war and peace.[38]

According to Neustadt, the nuclear paradox is this: "in a world of mutual superiority, neither nation can win a nuclear war, but each must be willing to risk losing."[39] To preserve values important to a nation, a leader must be willing "not to choose destruction, but nonetheless to choose the risk of destruction."[40] This President Kennedy was willing to do.

Neustadt contends that Kennedy followed a proper and responsible course of action during the crisis, despite the risk inherent in his action. If Kennedy had not taken a firm course of action, then the precarious status quo would have been jeopardized. Second, Kennedy's action gave warning to Khrushchev that he had miscalculated the determination of the United States. Third, if Kennedy had not responded forcefully, Khrushchev might not have believed that the United States would be willing to risk nuclear war to preserve Berlin. Finally, Kennedy's firm position in the crisis was a warning to the Soviets of the precariousness in the relations between the two nuclear superpowers. Thus, while the crisis over the missiles in Cuba was indeed risky, it was probably more manageable than a possible later crisis over Berlin where the United States did not have the comparative advantage in conventional forces.[41]

While Neustadt admires the decision of the President and Ex Com to implement a quarantine supported by the nuclear and conventional forces of the United States, he views this decision as a fortuitous coincidence of various factors of which the absence of any one might have led to an air strike. Hence, Professor Neustadt states:

The decision to blockade thus emerged as a collage. Its pieces included the initial decision by the President that something forceful had to be done; the resistance of Robert Kennedy, McNamara and Sorensen to the air strike; the relative distance between the President and the air strike advocates; and a probably inaccurate piece of information.[42]

While the decision to declare war rests constitutionally with Congress, during the missile crisis it rested for all practical purposes with the President. According to Neustadt, this is as it should be in a nuclear crisis, for formal congressional participation is both inconvenient and impractical. When a nuclear crisis occurs, secrecy, flexibility, and urgency make the President the nation's final arbiter.[43] Thus, in the case of the Cuban missile crisis, it was proper and essential that the warmaking power was tipped "all the way toward the President. . . . "[44]

One of the earliest full-length versions of the crisis of October 1962 was Henry M. Pachter's *Collision Course* (1963).[45] Although generally critical of Kennedy during his tenure as President, Pachter's interpretation of the crisis and the role of Kennedy in the crisis follows the traditional pattern of interpretation. While Pachter does not view the missile crisis as a turning point in East-West relations, he does claim that it was a dramatic climax in the Cold War. A former editor of *Dissent* magazine, Pachter covered the crisis as the U.N. correspondent for *Weltwoche*, a Zurich newspaper.

Unlike the traditionalists, Pachter ascribes the precipitation of the crisis to President Kennedy rather than to Chairman Khrushchev; however, like the traditionalists, he maintains that it was absolutely necessary for Kennedy to confront Khrushchev in order to restore U.S. defense commitments to credibility. "For the stability of peace and for the preservation of the balance of power, it was necessary for America to stand by all her promises."[46]

According to Pachter, the termination of the confrontation brought no fanfare, only a sigh of relief throughout the world. However, the successful resolution of the crisis did resolve grave doubts. It resolved the doubts about U.S. willpower; it resolved the doubts about the reasonableness of Khrushchev; and it resolved the doubts about the ability of statesmen to avoid a nuclear collision.[47]

The most novel aspect of Pachter's analysis of the crisis is his theory on the relationship of the two Khrushchev letters. The first letter received by the State Department on Friday evening, October 26, was a hastily written note, apparently composed personally by Khrushchev. This note basically sought a termination of the confrontation by having the Soviet Union withdraw its missiles from Cuba in exchange for the United States ending its blockade and pledging not to invade Cuba. A second formal letter, supposedly written by the professionals in the Kremlin, was received a few hours later. This second note called for exchanging the Soviet missiles in Cuba for the U.S. missiles in Turkey.[48]

Pachter contends that the two messages were received in the State Department in reverse order. Yet Pachter claims that the Chairman had written them both. The stronger formal note was written first, but the bureaucracy in the Soviet Foreign Office slowed its transmission. The hastily constructed informal note that does not mention the Turkish missiles was written second but was received first in the U.S. State Department because it was not sent through the Kremlin's bureaucratic channels, but rather it was submitted directly by Chairman Khrushchev to the State Department. The United States, therefore, had every right to dismiss the formal note on the Turkish bases and respond officially to the informal note.[49]

Pachter states that Kennedy displayed excellent leadership in the crisis. There was a distinct threat to the vital interests of the United States, and the President made his position known, a position that left avenues of retreat open to Khrushchev. Kennedy's action as well as his style restored U.S. confidence in its own power.[50] The President demonstrated that courage did not mean foolhardiness. With patience and decisiveness, Kennedy made certain that no reckless move would jeopardize the safety of the world. He led Khrushchev "close enough to the brink to make him understand that the abyss was no mirage."[51]

The Soviet Union attempted to change the status quo, which automatically led to the brink of nuclear war.[52] The status quo was essential to peace, and the only guardian of peace was power. It was a case of brinkmanship, of "realpolitik."[53] Only Kennedy and Khrushchev could have controlled the situation, which fortunately they did do. They were statesmen who took deterrence seriously; they acted responsibly and in so doing gave mankind a reprieve, for in the crisis mankind "went to the brink of Hell and came back again."[54]

The Missile Crisis (1966) by Elie Abel, former foreign correspondent for the *New York Times* and for the National Broadcasting Company, is a comprehensive presentation of crisis events that is based on extensive interviews with most of the administrative participants, particularly those in the State Department.[55] The book does not differ significantly in its day-to-day account of events from previous traditional sources, except it does reveal that there was much more traditional diplomacy being transacted than generally had been presumed prior to the book's publication. Abel's journalistic narrative is the presentation of those thirteen tension-filled days in October 1962 when "the young President played nuclear poker with Nikita Khrushchev and won."[56]

According to Abel, both Soviet and American intelligence agencies blundered from the outset. On the American side, the crucial error was that administration advisers refused to believe that the Soviet Union would put offensive missiles in Cuba. The advisers believed that Khrushchev, "being a rational man, would not take a step that seemed to Americans so dangerously irrational."[57] The crucial error of the Soviets was their failure "in grossly underestimating President Kennedy's readiness to act when challenged."[58] Khrushchev never questioned U.S. superiority in power; he only questioned the President's willingness to use it.[59] The fact that the President could not submit "to this direct intrusion of Soviet power into this hemisphere evidently escaped Khrushchev's notice or that of his advisers."[60]

While some revisionists have criticized the President for not suspending the quarantine when the Acting Secretary-General of the United Nations requested him to do so, Abel maintains that Kennedy had no choice but to retain the quarantine. To have accepted U Thant's request to suspend the quarantine "would pull the plug on the elaborate machinery of diplomatic and military pressure that he [the President] had just set in motion."[61]

Abel believes that President Kennedy responded splendidly to the crisis. While neither Kennedy nor Khrushchev instigated the nuclear poker situation, Kennedy behaved carefully and rationally, despite the irrationality of foreign politics. In the nuclear age, every President has the power to make war or to surrender vital interests of the United States. "Kennedy succeeded in steering a safe course between war and surrender."[62] He showed Khrushchev the edge of the nuclear abyss. Remembering that Khrushchev also was a politician, the President showed the Russian leader a way out without disgrace and without discredit.[63]

Edward Weintal and Charles Bartlett contend in *Facing the Brink* (1967) that the emplacement of missiles in Cuba was the decision of old revolutionaries like Khrushchev and Mikoyan and that Soviet experts on U.S. foreign policy were not consulted.[64] Khrushchev gambled in Cuba because he needed to score a victory in foreign policy to maintain Russian leadership in world communism and to counter the effects of failure in Russian agriculture.[65] Khrushchev believed that the United States would be so enthralled in the 1962 election campaign that if the missiles could be installed successfully before discovery, then the United States would accept a fait accompli.[66]

Against charges that President Kennedy overstated the perils of the crisis, Weintal and Bartlett claim that neither Kennedy nor his advisers had the advantage of hindsight and that at the time no one could be absolutely certain that Khrushchev would act rationally. Kennedy used the threat of "full retaliation," for he feared that the Soviets might attack Berlin, and the American defense of Berlin rested primarily on the power of nuclear weapons.[67]

Some critics of Kennedy's diplomacy in the crisis maintain that Kennedy was too anxious to deal with Khrushchev. Advocates of the right-wing interpretation have criticized Kennedy for not securing a more decisive triumph via the eradication of Castroism and communism in Cuba by use of an air strike or an invasion. Against these charges, Weintal and Bartlett contend that Kennedy could not "mortify the man [Khrushchev] and hope to deal constructively with him later."[68] The Cuban crisis, Weintal and Bartlett conclude, was Kennedy's greatest success in the foreign policy arena.[69]

The problems involved in the implementation of the principles of crisis management and the improvisation by Kennedy of a coercive strategy are analyzed by Alexander L. George in his essay, "The Cuban Missile Crisis, 1962," which appeared in *The Limits of Coercive Diplomacy* by Alexander L. George, David K. Hall, and William E. Simons (1970).[70] George, who is a political scientist at Stanford University, explains Kennedy's handling of the crisis as a movement from the "try-and-see" approach to the "tacit-ultimatum" approach. He demonstrates how difficult it is to apply the coersive diplomacy principles of bargaining, negotiation, compromise, and threat to a crisis situation even when a country possesses military superiority.

According to George, the emplacement of Soviet missiles in Cuba represented an affront to the President as well as to major U.S. interests. Kennedy had no other option than to respond. "Moreover, for the President to retreat from the explicit commitment [to act if missiles were introduced into Cuba] . . . would have eroded all U.S. commitments and invited Khrushchev and others to question Kennedy's future credibility."[71]

President Kennedy believed, according to George, that he had to respond in a manner that involved the prestige of Khrushchev. Any diplomatic action that did not involve Khrushchev's prestige was considered likely to be ineffectual. Thus Kennedy accepted the quarantine because he believed that it would strike at Khrushchev's prestige sufficiently enough to force the Chairman to retreat before the missiles became operational.[72]

The problem of the blockade, a weak form of coercive diplomacy, was that it was conceived without any necessary connection to securing the withdrawal of the missiles in Cuba, according to George. Kennedy was "caught squarely between the requirements of crisis control and those of [firm] coercive diplomacy."[73] Hence, Kennedy switched from the "try-and-see" approach to the "ultimatum" approach on Friday, October 26. George concludes that this switch from the blockade to naval harassment of Soviet submarines via shadowing them may well have convinced Khrushchev of Kennedy's determination.[74] This switch from crisis control and weak coercion to firm coercive diplomacy resulted in the resolution of the Cuban missile crisis.

How well did Kennedy perform in the missile crisis? George claims that while Kennedy's actions did involve the risk of war, the President did not behave recklessly to increase its probability. He further claims that

there is nothing in the available materials to suggest that the President's judgment was distorted by an emotional response to being deceived by Khrushchev, by adherence to an extreme Cold War image of the Soviets, or by a desire to punish Khrushchev for his misbehavior—although certainly the President did feel it necessary to correct his opponent's mistaken notion that he lacked determination.[75]

Despite the inherent conflict between crisis management and coercive diplomacy, George concludes that "Kennedy dealt with the problems of the strategy of coercive diplomacy skillfully."[76] Yet, he adds with a note of caution, "there was no guarantee that he would and no way of predicting."[77]

Like the traditionalists writing from the perspective of the participants, the traditionalists writing from the observers' viewpoint also reach consensus in several areas. In concurrence with the participants, the observers believe that both U.S. and Soviet intelligence experts grossly miscalculated the response of their adversary. The Russians assumed that President Kennedy would accept operational offensive nuclear missiles in Cuba as a fait accompli (Weintal), and, therefore, the Soviets erroneously miscalculated the determined response of Kennedy and the U.S. government (Neustadt, Abel). In similar manner, the intelligence experts assumed that Chairman Khrushchev, as a rational being, would not undertake such a risky course of action as emplacing nuclear missiles in Cuba because such action would be interpreted as irrational by the United States; hence, a rational man would not initiate such an irrational operation (Abel). Since the Russians had never before permitted offensive nuclear missiles outside the Soviet Union, U.S. intelligence inaccurately assumed that such a policy was a permanent fixture in Soviet foreign policy (Sidey).

The Soviets primarily sought to effect a favorable change in the balance of power; they sought to change the status quo strategically and/or politically (Alsop, Sidey, Neustadt, Carleton, Pachter, Abel, George). The Russian leadership covertly emplaced missiles in Cuba to compensate for the missile gap that favored the United States (Carleton) and to reassert their authority and prestige as the leaders in international communism (Weintal).

The Soviet ballistic missiles in Cuba were an affront to the vital interests of the United States and to the President (George). Kennedy had to respond firmly to the Soviet challenge in order to preserve world peace, American values, and the delicate balance of power (Alsop, Sidey, Carleton, Neustadt, Pachter); if the President had not responded staunchly, the credibility of U.S. defense commitments would have eroded (Pachter,

George), and the United States would have become a paper tiger, a second-class power (Alsop).

Whether the quarantine decision was fortuitous by accident (Neustadt) and whether it was only a weak form of coercive diplomacy (George) is debatable, but the observers are in agreement that the President did ascend the ladder of coercion to the point of brinkmanship (Carleton, Neustadt, Pachter, Weintal, George). Kennedy led Khrushchev to the brink of the nuclear abyss so that the Chairman could see the lunacy of a thermonuclear showdown (Carleton, Pachter, Abel). In so doing, the President responsibly risked destruction to preserve American values and world peace (Neustadt).

Despite the risks involved, President Kennedy pioneered the way in nuclear confrontations; he demonstrated exceptional skills in crisis management (Neustadt) and in effective coercive diplomacy (George). The President controlled the crisis by his combining deliberation with planning, toughness with flexibility, and coercion with caution (Alsop, Sidey, Neustadt). He made no reckless moves (Pachter) and behaved rationally despite the irrationality normally present in foreign affairs (Abel). In the final analysis, President Kennedy and the members of Ex Com performed superbly during those critical thirteen days of October 1962 (Sidey). Kennedy followed a relatively safe course between war and surrender (Abel), and, thus, he demonstrated an exceptionally rare understanding and use of the Presidency (Sidey).

According to the observers writing in the traditional interpretative mode, the Cuban missile crisis was the high-water mark in the Kennedy Presidency (Carleton). The crisis was Kennedy's greatest success (Weintal), and it was a dramatic climax in the Cold War (Pachter). The successful termination of the crisis resolved doubts about U.S. determination and doubts about the ability of statesmen to avoid a nuclear holocaust (Pachter). Détente ensued with Khrushchev following the path of peaceful coexistence and Kennedy harmonizing U.S. foreign policy with reality (Carleton). And, finally, the United States and its young President were held in rare esteem as defenders of the free world by freedom-loving people everywhere (Sidey).

NOTES

1. Stewart Alsop and Charles Bartlett, "In Time of Crisis," *Saturday Evening Post*, December 8, 1962, pp. 16–20.

2. *Ibid.*

3. *Ibid.*, p. 18.

4. *Ibid.*

5. *Ibid.*

6. *Ibid.*, p. 20.

7. *Ibid.*

8. *Ibid.*

9. Hugh Sidey, *John F. Kennedy, President*, 2nd ed. (New York: Atheneum, 1964).

10. Hugh Sidey, "The Presidency: The Classic Use of the Great Office," *Life*, November 22, 1968, p. 4; reprinted in *J. F. Kennedy and Presidential Power*, ed. Earl Latham (Lexington, Mass.: D.C. Health, 1972).

11. Sidey, *John F. Kennedy*, pp. 324–25.

12. *Ibid.*, p. 333.

13. Sidey, "The Presidency," p. 4.

14. Sidey, *John F. Kennedy*, p. 338.

15. *Ibid.*

16. Sidey, "The Presidency," p. 4.

17. *Ibid.*

18. *Ibid.*

19. Sidey, *John F. Kennedy*, p. 347.

20. *Ibid.*, p. 348.

21. William G. Carleton, "Kennedy in History: An Early Appraisal," in *The Politics of John F. Kennedy*, ed. Edmund S. Ions (New York: Barnes and Noble, 1967); originally published in *The Antioch Review* 24 (Fall 1964): 277–99.

22. Carleton, "Kennedy," *Politics*, p. 215.

23. *Ibid.*, p. 212.

24. *Ibid.*

25. *Ibid.*, p. 210.

26. *Ibid.*, p. 216.

27. *Ibid.*

28. *Ibid.*, p. 217.

29. *Ibid.*

30. *Ibid.*

31. Richard E. Neustadt, *Presidential Power: The Politics of Leadership* (New York: John Wiley, 1960); "Afterword: JFK" (1968).

32. *Ibid.*, p. 200.
33. *Ibid.*, p. 210.
34. *Ibid.*, pp. 203–04.
35. *Ibid.*, p. 207.
36. *Ibid.*, p. 208.
37. Richard E. Neustadt and Graham T. Allison, "Afterword" to *Thirteen Days: A Memoir of the Cuban Missile Crisis* by Robert F. Kennedy (New York: W. W. Norton, 1971).
38. *Ibid.*, p. 109.
39. *Ibid.*, pp. 114–15.
40. *Ibid.*, p. 115.
41. *Ibid.*, pp. 115–16.
42. *Ibid.*, p. 130. The inaccurate piece of information to which Neustadt refers is Lieutenant General Sweeney's statement to the President that an air strike could not be surgical. Neustadt believes that the surgical air strike option could have been chosen with high confidence. On this issue, Neustadt differs with the other traditional writers.
43. *Ibid.*, pp. 140–45.
44. *Ibid.*, p. 145.
45. Henry M. Pachter, *Collision Course: The Cuban Missile Crisis and Coexistence* (New York: Frederick A. Praeger, 1963). For a highly unfavorable assessment of Kennedy by Pachter, see "JFK as an Equestrian Statue: On Myth and Mythmakers," *Salmagundi* 1 (Spring 1966): 3–26.
46. Pachter, *Collision Course*, p. 53.
47. *Ibid.*, p. 59.
48. *Ibid.*, p. 66.
49. *Ibid.*, pp. 67–68.
50. *Ibid.*, pp. 86–87.
51. *Ibid.*, p. 88.
52. *Ibid.*, p. 105.
53. *Ibid.*, p. 93.
54. *Ibid.*, p. 59.
55. Elie Abel, *The Missile Crisis* (Philadelphia: J. B. Lippincott, 1966). This book was republished in 1969 as *The Missiles of October: The Story of the Cuban Missile Crisis, 1962* (London: MacGibbon and Kee, 1969).
56. Abel, *Missile Crisis*, book jacket.
57. *Ibid.*, p. 34.
58. *Ibid.*
59. *Ibid.*, p. 36.
60. *Ibid.*, p. 40.
61. *Ibid.*, p. 150.

62. *Ibid.*, p. 215.

63. *Ibid.*

64. Edward Weintal and Charles Bartlett, *Facing the Brink: An Intimate Study of Crisis Diplomacy* (New York: Charles Scribner's Sons, 1967), p. 59.

65. *Ibid.*

66. *Ibid.*, pp. 55–58.

67. *Ibid.*, p. 67.

68. *Ibid.*, p. 68.

69. *Ibid.*, p. 14.

70. Alexander L. George, "The Cuban Missile Crisis, 1962," in *The Limits of Coercive Diplomacy: Laos, Cuba, Vietnam*, eds. Alexander L. George, David K. Hall, and William E. Simons (Boston: Little, Brown, 1971). See also by the same author, "The Cuban Missile Crisis, 1962," in *Deterrence in American Foreign Policy: Theory and Practice*, Alexander L. George and Richard Smoke (New York: Columbia University Press, 1974).

71. George, *Coercive Diplomacy*, p. 93.

72. *Ibid.*, p. 89.

73. *Ibid.*, p. 95.

74. *Ibid.*, p. 96.

75. *Ibid.*, p. 94.

76. *Ibid.*, p. 136.

77. *Ibid.*

this unwillingness lies not so much with individuals or with political parties, according to Lowenthal, but with the U.S. philosophy of international affairs. The United States is afraid to coerce for moral ends; it is afraid to utilize retaliation, that form of coercion which is essential to survival. Thus, fearing strong coercive measures, the United States secured the removal of nuclear missiles from Cuba by making a concession to the Soviets in the form of a noninvasion pledge, a pledge "that will assist the growth of Communist military power and subversion in this hemisphere."[6]

This same viewpoint was reiterated in the ever-popular *Reader's Digest* in November 1964 by Richard M. Nixon.[7] In an article entitled "Cuba, Castro and John F. Kennedy," of which a succinct portion pertains to the Cuban missile crisis, Nixon states that the President's advisers by their suggestion that Kennedy not take strong, decisive measures against Cuba in the form of an air strike or an invasion "enabled the United States to pull defeat out of the jaws of victory."[8]

Nixon contends that the lack of firmness in U.S. foreign policy turned Khrushchev's nuclear missile gamble into a victory for the Kremlin. While offensive missiles apparently were removed, defensive missiles were allowed to remain. Together with continuing shiploads of Soviet arms to Cuba, the defensive missiles made Cuba the strongest military power in the Western Hemisphere with the exception of the United States and Canada. And the commitment of the United States to a no-invasion pledge only strengthened the Cuban position.[9]

The first detailed right-wing analysis of the missile crisis appeared in the 1963 winter issue of *Orbis* in an article by Robert D. Crane entitled "The Cuban Crisis: A Strategic Analysis of American and Soviet Policy."[10] Crane's thesis is that President Kennedy's apparent lack of resoluteness confirmed the Soviets' decision to emplace missiles in Cuba and that the President's policy of moderation during the crisis and accommodation after the crisis may have convinced the Soviets that they could take similar military action elsewhere under more favorable circumstances.

Crane cites three occasions prior to the missile buildup in Cuba on which the President demonstrated his lack of resolve.

First, in April 1961, Kennedy withdrew crucial air support from the exiled Cubans in the ill-fated Bay of Pigs invasion. Second, in June 1961 in Vienna, Kennedy agreed with Premier Khrushchev to the neutralization of Laos, which was tantamount to the abandonment of that country to communism. Third, in August 1961, Kennedy strenuously objected to the erection of the Berlin Wall, but he failed to take any action.[11] These events, according to Crane, convinced the Russians that "the United States would not respond with military force to the creation of an offensive Soviet base in Cuba."[12]

Granted that the Soviets believed that the United States would not respond militarily to the Russian scheme to emplace missiles in Cuba, why did the Soviets want to establish a strategic weapons base there anyway? According to Crane, the objectives of this strategic venture were twofold. First, the Soviets sought to change rapidly the nuclear balance of power in their favor so as to "facilitate more effective bargaining with the United States in other areas of the world"[13] Second, the Soviets sought to "overawe the 'colossus of the north' in its own hemisphere" so as to prove to the entire world that "the tide of history . . . [is] flowing decisively and irrevocably in favor of world communism."[14] That is, the Soviet objectives were strategic and ideological.

Crane contends that President Kennedy gave only the appearance of firmness in his response to the crisis. Considering the overpowering military superiority of the United States and the extent of the Soviet provocation, the United States surprisingly exhibited restraint in its use of military force.[15] The United States never threatened any action more stringent than simply tightening the blockade.[16] Hence, Crane believes that the Soviets emerged from the crisis "with no more appreciation of American resolve than when they entered it."[17]

Following the immediate period of confrontation, the United States adopted a policy of accommodation. Retreating from his statement of October 22 that the United States would not terminate its quarantine until all offensive weapons had been withdrawn from Cuba under United Nations supervision, President Kennedy terminated the naval quarantine on November 20. He did so in response to the Soviet withdrawal of the missiles; however in doing so, the President ended the quarantine without United Nations inspection and with Ilyushin bombers still in Cuba.[18]

According to Crane, when the crisis was over, the United States adopted a policy of minimum risk and maximum security. That is, the United States followed a policy of moderation in response to Soviet initiatives. Crane concludes that such a policy is erroneous and should be replaced by a policy that pursues "the long-range strategy of reversing the entire course of the communists' global strategy and, ultimately, of forcing them to abandon their ideology."[19]

James Daniel and John Hubbell collaborated in 1963 in writing the first full-length book on the Cuban missile crisis. Dedicated to Major Rudolf Anderson, Jr., the only casualty in the confrontation, *Strike in the West* is a moderate right-wing interpretation of the crisis, emphasizing the military aspects of the U.S. response to the Soviet ballistic missiles in Cuba in 1962.[20]

Daniel and Hubbell charge that U.S. intelligence grossly miscalculated Soviet foreign policy by confidently assuming that the Soviet Union would not emplace offensive missiles in Cuba because of the highly volatile nature of Fidel Castro.[21] The State Department erred in brushing aside early reports of the Soviet offensive military buildup in Cuba, and the administration erred in uncritically accepting Khrushchev's assurances that Russia would not send any weapons to Cuba that could be used to attack the United States.[22] The miscalculation was so incredible that the full extent of Russian military deployment in Cuba, apart from the number of MRBMs and IRBMs, will never be disclosed because such a revelation would "shock the American public and raise questions in Congress as to how the administration had managed for so long not to see so much."[23] By implication, therefore, Daniel and Hubbell charge the Kennedy administration with conspiracy to conceal information about the missile crisis.

Daniel and Hubbell contend that the Soviet talk about settling the Berlin question was simply a diversion to keep the administration's attention on Berlin while the Soviet Union made Cuba militarily impregnable. "Under cover of Russia's noisy threats in Berlin, the Soviet strike in the West would have achieved its aim."[24] The aim, according to Daniel and Hubbell, was nothing less than a drastic alteration of the strategic balance of world power.[25]

Chairman Khrushchev, Daniel and Hubbell claim, assumed that the United States would not respond militarily to defend its interests. Khrushchev believed that the United States had neither the fortitude for power politics nor the nerve to use its military power. Hence, the Chairman believed that he could effectively change the balance of power with ease by emplacing nuclear offensive missiles in Cuba.[26]

The discovery of the missiles in Cuba via Major Anderson's reconnaissance flight presented President Kennedy with two basic options. Either he could do nothing and accept a new balance of power, or he could respond and risk initiating a general war.[27] Not to respond would amount to surrender; such would reduce U.S. credibility and destroy the effectiveness of NATO and the OAS. "The cold war would be over. Russia would have won."[28]

The President firmly responded to the crisis and was prepared to use the equivalent of 30 billion tons of TNT against the Soviet Union.[29] However, while simultaneously exerting such pressure upon the Soviet Union with firm resolution, Kennedy also exercised restraint by giving Khrushchev time to reflect and to withdraw at each stage of the crisis.[30] Such a combination led to the termination of the crisis. "The United States had boldly asserted its will—and its might—in the Nuclear Age. The enemy had refused the challenge."[31]

While many interpreters regard the crisis as a victory for President Kennedy and the United States, Daniel and Hubbell ask: Where are the fruits of the victory? The crisis had raised high hopes of liberation, but the dictatorship of Fidel Castro still is entrenched in Cuba. Thousands of combat-ready Russian troops, as well as significant military equipment, still remain in Cuba. Are these the fruits of victory?[32]

There are, nonetheless, some important and positive aspects that emerged from the crisis, according to Daniel and Hubbell. If the United States was only a paper tiger before the crisis, it was now a paper tiger with nuclear teeth. If the United States or its allies doubted the U.S. ability to repel aggression, it w .

now evident that the United States could repel aggression with its combined conventional and nuclear power. Finally, if the Soviets thought that the Americans would panic under nuclear blackmail, it was now demonstrated that neither the Americans nor their allies would panic under Soviet nuclear threats.[33]

In *The Leadership of President Kennedy* (1964), retired Major General Thomas A. Lane portrays President Kennedy as a young man of personal charm who was prematurely forced by an ambitious family to seek the presidency for which he had no previous experience or qualifications.[34] This lack of experience demonstrated itself in the President's lack of leadership before and during the Cuban missile crisis; it was leadership by retreat and failure.

According to Lane, Premier Khrushchev sought to emplace missiles in Cuba so as to assist Castro in consolidating his dictatorship of the island before the disillusioned Cuban populace revolted against him.[35] To secure the Castro regime, Khrushchev decided that is was necessary to use the presence of Soviet power to intimidate potential Cuban army rebels.[36] While Khrushchev knew that the Soviet presence in Cuba would be a sensitive issue, he also knew that the President and his advisers were visionary and impractical young men who were fearful of confrontations and who were strongly disposed to delay and appease.[37] Khrushchev, therefore, believed that the emplacement of nuclear missiles in Cuba would not be a dangerous venture for the Soviet Union.[38]

Lane contends that a strong President would have invoked the Monroe Doctrine at the first sign of any Soviet presence in Cuba, but Kennedy initially failed to exercise firm leadership out of a fear that any firm action might precipitate nuclear war.[39] The President's preconception that the Chairman would act moderately in support of Castro "paralyzed his capacity to be objective."[40] Thus Kennedy permitted the Soviet commitment to Castro to increase.

Lane claims that the President's concern that the crisis might lead to nuclear war betrays the amateurish quality of Kennedy's leadership. "To suppose that the Soviet leaders would prefer nuclear war to withdrawal from Cuba is to confess profound ignorance of power, politics, and the enemy."[41] Because of

U.S. nuclear superiority, any fear that the Soviet Union would resort to thermonuclear war was entirely imaginary.[42]

Lane believes that Kennedy had the same information on the Soviet buildup in Cuba as that which was available to Senator Keating. The President, however, had hoped that he would not have to take any action in Cuba until after the election. When Kennedy realized that inaction would be dangerous politically to him, he responded to the critical situation.[43] It was simply a case of "practiced reaction to political necessity."[44]

While the President's address of October 22 raised hopes that U.S. leadership had at last decided to challenge Soviet imperialism, such hopes were in vain. In terminating the crisis, Kennedy followed a policy of accommodation. By his noninvasion pledge, the President gave the Soviets what they wanted most: "the security of the Communist beachhead in Cuba."[45] Furthermore, the President compromised the strength of the U.S. position in the world by subsequently removing its missiles from Turkey and Italy.[46]

Lane concludes his remarks thusly: "The unsung hero of the missile crisis was Senator Keating . . . who built the fire in the American people which forced President Kennedy to act. Without his prudent and persistent warning, the United States might today be facing intermediate range missiles in Cuba."[47]

Malcolm E. Smith reiterates Lane's basic argument in *Kennedy's Thirteen Greatest Mistakes in the White House* (1968).[48] While giving credit to the President for his firmness in responding eventually to the crisis and for saving the United States from Russian nuclear blackmail and possibly nuclear attack, Smith claims that the President gravely erred by his initial inaction and failure to appraise properly intelligence evidence on the buildup of the Soviet presence in Cuba.[49] Having permitted the introduction of nuclear missiles into Cuba, Kennedy was forced by the gravity of the situation to respond boldly and decisively to save the United States from disaster.[50]

Smith accuses the President of intentionally ignoring the Cuban situation. The administration sought to prevent Cuba from becoming the foremost issue in the political campaign of 1962.[51] Thus Kennedy refused in the summer of 1962 to invoke the Monroe Doctrine to protect the nation, "a tragic and nearly fatal mistake."[52] Finally, the President was forced by political considerations to give attention to the Soviet buildup in Cuba before the people went to the polls.[53] Ironically, Kennedy's courageous confrontation with Khrushchev secured a Democratic victory in the November elections.[54]

While the President was courageous at the height of the crisis, he adopted a policy of concession before the crisis ended. According to Smith, the United States unnecessarily promised not to invade Cuba or overthrow Castro by force. The United States also paid a high price in promising to withdraw missiles from Turkey, Italy, and England.[55] Yet Kennedy's greatest mistake in his policy of concession was to retreat from his original position of demanding inspection of Cuba after the missiles purportedly were withdrawn, for intermediate-range nuclear missiles are still hidden in Cuban caves.[56]

According to the traditionalists, the signing of the Nuclear Test Ban Treaty was an important by-product of the Cuban missile crisis; some even claim that it was President Kennedy's greatest accomplishment. Smith takes a contrary view of this in insisting that it was perhaps Kennedy's greatest mistake. The treaty failed to deter the proliferation of nuclear weapons to other nations while it prevented the United States from conducting high altitude tests.[57] As a result of the treaty, the Soviet Union advanced toward nuclear superiority.[58] While there was no missile gap unfavorable to the United States in 1960 as Kennedy charged, there is now "a real missile gap . . . impending as a result of President Kennedy's decisions."[59]

Dean Acheson, former Secretary of State in the Truman administration, was a nonadministration, part-time participant in some of the deliberations of Ex Com during the 1962 October crisis. Following the publication of Robert Kennedy's *Thirteen Days*, Acheson discussed his differences with the Attorney General in an article for *Esquire* entitled "Dean Acheson's Version of Robert Kennedy's Version of the Cuban Missile Affair" (1969).[60] Acheson, who was a hawk in the Ex Com meetings, praises the President for his leadership, firmness, and judgment during the confrontation but claims that the President was helped "by the luck of Khrushchev's befuddlement and loss of nerve."[61]

Acheson believes that Khrushchev's objectives in Cuba were threefold. First, the Premier sought to increase the Soviet Union's first-strike capacity against the United States by as much as 50 percent. Second, Khrushchev sought to discredit the United States in the Western Hemisphere by the Soviet Union's show of military power. Finally, Khrushchev sought to discredit the United States in Europe and Asia by forcing the United States to make concessions in these areas in exchange for the withdrawal of Soviet ballistic missiles from Cuba.[62]

Acheson maintains that the threat posed by the Soviet missiles on the island republic increased U.S. vulnerability to attack, for the shorter range missiles in Cuba could be as effective and as powerful as the intercontinental missiles in the Soviet Union. Such a change in the nuclear balance of power required the President to respond firmly. To have taken a passive position in this situation would have caused the United States to lose the confidence of the countries in the Western Hemisphere as well as those in Western Europe.[63]

At the time of the crisis, Acheson rejected Robert Kennedy's analogy that an attack on the nuclear missile installations in Cuba would be a "Pearl Harbor in reverse." At Pearl Harbor, the Japanese without warning or provocation attacked the U.S. fleet thousands of miles from its continental base. In the Cuban situation, however, the Soviet Union had installed lethal weapons only ninety miles from the U.S. coastline in utter disregard of the 140-year-old Monroe Doctrine. Furthermore, President Kennedy had reiterated the Monroe Doctrine warning only weeks before the discovery of nuclear missiles in Cuba.[64]

During the crisis deliberations, Acheson supported an air strike on the Soviet missile installations. He considered the blockade or quarantine an ineffective instrument, for it was a method "of keeping things out, not getting things out, of a beleaguered spot."[65] The quarantine was directed not at the controller of the nuclear weapons in Cuba but at the host of the controller. The quarantine, therefore, left the Soviet Union in control of the crisis.[66]

As for Ex Com, Acheson considered it a perversion of the National Security Council. The members had little or no knowledge of either military or diplomatic affairs.[67] The sessions were "repetitive, leaderless, and [a] waste of time."[68]

Acheson concludes his article by restating his position that the proper course of action would have been an air strike on the missile installations. He claims that the President's attempt to get Khrushchev to retreat by sending messages was a "gamble to the point of recklessness."[69] While he communicated with Khrushchev, the work on the missile sites was continuing uninterrupted. Luck, however, triumphed, and President Kennedy succeeded in terminating the confrontation.[70]

Born in the United States of Latin American parentage, Mario Lazo practiced law in Havana for forty years until his law firm of Lazo and Cubas was destroyed by Fidel Castro following the Bay of Pigs invasion. Imprisoned by Castro, Lazo eventually was released and returned to the United States where he wrote *Dagger in the Heart* (1968).[71] In his book Lazo presents a far-right-wing interpretation of the failure of U.S. foreign policy to prevent the capitulation of Cuba to communism. Lazo's thesis is that the liberal political leaders in the United States literally handed Cuba over to communism by their policies of caution, restraint, and compromise.

Lazo lays the blame for the Soviet introduction of missiles into Cuba on President Kennedy, for it was the President's inexperience and his tendency to vacillate that convinced Chairman Khrushchev that his scheme could be executed successfully.[72] Khrushchev was convinced that he was dealing "with an inexperienced young leader who could be intimidated and blackmailed."[73] Evidence to substantiate such confidence was abundant. Kennedy had done nothing when the communists erected the Berlin Wall. He had agreed with Khrushchev to the bogus neutralization of Laos, and while he was adverturesome enough to permit the Bay of Pigs invasion, he was not bold enough to provide the essential air support required for success.[74]

Lazo contends that the Ex Com deliberations during the crisis were a repetition of the Bay of Pigs discussions, with the President demonstrating his usual tendency to temporize and back away from difficult decisions.[75] Kennedy sided with the

liberals who opposed any action that would provoke or humiliate the Russians.[76] Thus the President rejected the conservatives' request for strong action to "eliminate the threat posed
by Khrushchev's nuclear blackmail . . . [and] to get rid of Castro and Communism in Cuba."[77]

According to Lazo, the Cuban missile crisis was a power confrontation between the United States and the Soviet Union in
which the trump cards were held by the President.[78] The conventional and nuclear military power of the United States was
incomparably superior to that of the Soviet Union, and both
Kennedy and Khrushchev knew this as a fact. Because the nuclear strike capability of the Russians was negligible, the Americans could have destroyed every significant population center
and military installation in the Soviet Union within a couple of
hours. Yet the President refused to play his trump cards.[79]

President Kennedy, in his exchange of agreements with Premier Khrushchev terminating the confrontation, abandoned
Cuba to communism and, according to Lazo, Kennedy was
aware of what he was doing when he handed Cuba over to the
communist system.[80] In his agreement with Khrushchev, President Kennedy made a mockery of his promises given after the
Bay of Pigs invasion that the United States would never abandon Cuba to communism.[81]

The end result of the missile crisis was to give communism
a beachhead in Cuba against which the President promised not
to take any substantive action.[82] For the Cuban patriots, however, the noninvasion pledge meant more than a hands-off
policy; it signified to them "American intervention to protect
Castro and the Soviet forces in Cuba."[83]

The Cuban missile crisis was not President Kennedy's finest
hour, nor was it a victory for Kennedy, according to Lazo. The
ultimate result of the U.S.-Soviet confrontation was "a calami-
tous defeat for the United States and Latin America, and therefore for the entire Free World."[84]

Paul D. Bethel, a former press attaché to the American Embassy in Havana and a former political prisoner under Castro,
presents another far-right-wing interpretation of the Cuban
missile crisis in his book, *The Losers* (1969).[85] Bethel's thesis is
that President Kennedy intentionally and erroneously por-

trayed the crisis as a doomsday confrontation so that he could abandon Cuba to communism in exchange for rapprochement with the Soviet Union. Bethel even goes so far as to conclude that possibly "the two nuclear powers had cooperated in an unbelievably cynical deception."[86]

Bethel charges that President Kennedy and his isolationist liberals, the losers, virtually invited the Soviets into Cuba.[87] In the weeks and months prior to the October crisis, Kennedy remained aloof from the public and congressional clamor for action and clearly implied that he would not interfere with the Soviet intervention in Cuba unless the United States was placed under the threat of imminent attack.[88]

Bethel also charges that Robert Kennedy, acting as if he were an Assistant President, set the tone of the Ex Com discussions by refusing to consider seriously any proposal that involved an air strike on the missile installations. The liberals of the New Frontier insisted that an air strike would have to be followed by an invasion, something the administration refused to contemplate.[89] While the Attorney General manipulated the Ex Com deliberations, the President controlled information to the press so as "to prevent any public reaction which might force him into a more militant position."[90]

According to Bethel, President Kennedy's address to the world of October 22, 1962, "amounted to little more than an invitation to the Soviets to remove their missiles from Cuba."[91] Despite the drama-charged atmosphere, the speech was mild, for Kennedy's deeper intent was to invite the Russians to move toward rapprochement with the United States. The President achieved his intent in his letter of capitulation of October 27 to Khrushchev. Therein, the President offered to trade Cuba to the Soviet Union in exchange for a rapprochement.[92] Khrushchev therefore secured by the President's capitulation what he sought when he decided to emplace missiles in Cuba—namely, an ironclad guarantee of the territorial integrity of Cuba by the United States.[93]

In conclusion, Bethel contends that the Sorensen-Kennedy-Schlesinger presentation of the missile crisis is one of the greatest deceptions of the modern world. To set the record straight, Bethel enumerates the "facts" of the crisis:

(1) the range of missiles withdrawn from Cuba deflates the doomsday interpretation placed upon this event by the New Frontier; (2) Khrushchev abruptly stopped threatening President Kennedy with war over West Berlin; (3) the Democrats won the 1962 elections; (4) President Kennedy removed Jupiter missiles from Turkey and Italy; (5) President Kennedy achieved a dubious claim to courage and leadership of the free world and set about intensifying rapprochement with an enemy who had just defeated him; (6) the Bay of Pigs prisoners were released, but the people of Cuba were cynically consigned to the straight-jacket of a Communist state; (7) Cuba today is Communism's most important base for subversion outside the Soviet Union; (8) IRBM's may still be in Cuba, siloed and ready. If this point was indeed known to President Kennedy, it alone explains the other seven.[94]

While the interpreters of the right-wing perspective of the Cuban missile crisis do not form as cohesive an interpretation as the traditionalists, they do agree on a number of issues. For example, they generally agree that President Kennedy partially is responsible for the crisis because his lack of resolve and firmness in foreign policy convinced Khrushchev that he could succeed in his nuclear venture in Cuba. Khrushchev had witnessed the President's lack of resolve in the building of the Berlin Wall, in the neutralization of Laos, and in the ill-fated Bay of Pigs invasion (Crane, Lazo, Bethel). The Premier, therefore, unimpressed with Kennedy's leadership, believed that he could intimidate and blackmail the President (Lowenthal, Lazo). Khrushchev undoubtedly believed that the United States would avoid a confrontation and would not utilize its superior military power to defend its interest (Crane, Daniel, Lane, Lazo).

As to why the Soviets sought to emplace missiles in Cuba, the right-wing interpreters are divided. The more restrained right-wing perspective is that the Soviets intended to change the strategic balance of world power (Daniel, Acheson). The far-right-wing viewpoint, however, is that the Soviet Union sought to strengthen its ideological position in the world by successfully strengthening Castro's dictatorship and firmly entrenching communism in the Western Hemisphere (Lane, Lazo, Bethel).

In similar manner, the right-wing interpreters are divided over the reason for Kennedy's reacting to the crisis. According to the restrained right-wing interpretation, the President responded to the Soviet offensive nuclear intrusion into the Western Hemisphere because to have done nothing would have been tantamount to surrender; it would have utterly destroyed the credibility of the United States and the effectiveness of both NATO and the OAS (Daniel, Acheson). The far-right-wing interpreters take exception to this perspective. According to their viewpoint, Kennedy reacted to the Soviet military buildup in Cuba only after he assessed that to do so was politically advantageous to him and the Democrats in the 1962 campaign; it was a simple case of practiced reaction to political necessity (Lane, Smith, Bethel).

While some of the right-wing interpreters contend that President Kennedy reacted firmly to the crisis in the manner of a strong man who had been pushed too far by a bully and, thus, saved America from nuclear blackmail (Daniel, Smith), most of the individuals writing from this perspective accuse the President of lacking leadership and bold initiative (Lowenthal, Nixon, Crane, Lane, Acheson, Lazo, Bethel). Considering the extent of the Soviet provocation in Cuba, Kennedy acted with extreme restraint, and, in so doing, he came very close to retracting the Monroe Doctrine (Lowenthal). Despite the absolute improbability of a nuclear war, the President's fear of it paralyzed him to such an extent that he refused to take any coercive action that might provoke or humiliate Khrushchev (Lane, Lazo). The caution, restraint, and compromising spirit of the President and the liberal isolationists of Ex Com demonstrated the amateurish leadership of the United States (Lane, Acheson, Lazo). In the end, Kennedy's lack of leadership in utilizing an air strike or an invasion during the crisis gave Khrushchev what he wanted by his Cuban venture—namely, a communist beachhead in the Western Hemisphere (Lane, Lazo). By his policy of accommodation, the President abandoned Cuba to communism in exchange for a rapprochement with the Soviet Union (Bethel). By the same policy, Kennedy withdrew U.S. missiles in Turkey, Italy, and England (Lane, Smith).

Unlike the traditionalists, the right wing finds the fruits of defeat rather than those of victory in the termination of the U.S.-Soviet confrontation. By his no-invasion pledge, President

Kennedy guaranteed the territorial integrity of Cuba and the successful entrenchment of communism (Lowenthal, Nixon, Lane, Smith, Lazo, Bethel). Fidel Castro remained firmly in control of the island's destiny (Daniel, Bethel), and the Russians in combat-readiness remained there as well as significant military equipment, including possibly nuclear missiles (Nixon, Daniel, Bethel). Finally, as part of the new rapprochement between the United States and the Soviet Union, President Kennedy signed a deadly compromising document, the Nuclear Test Ban Treaty (Smith).

NOTES

1. David Lowenthal, "U.S. Cuban Policy: Illusion and Reality," *National Review*, January 29, 1963, pp. 61–63.

2. *Ibid.*, p. 62.

3. *Ibid.*, p. 63.

4. *Ibid.*, p. 62.

5. *Ibid.*, p. 63.

6. *Ibid.*, p. 61.

7. Richard M. Nixon, "Cuba, Castro and John F. Kennedy," *Reader's Digest*, November 1964, pp. 283–300. For a more moderate interpretation, see Henry A. Kissinger, "Reflections on Cuba," *The Reporter*, November 22, 1962, pp. 21–24.

8. Nixon, "Cuba," p. 297.

9. *Ibid.*

10. Robert D. Crane, "The Cuban Crisis: A Strategic Analysis of American and Soviet Policy," *Orbis* 6 (Winter 1963): 528–63. See also by the same author, "The Sino-Soviet Dispute on War and the Cuban Crisis," *Orbis* 7 (Fall 1964): 537–49.

11. Crane, "The Cuban Crisis," pp. 532–33.

12. *Ibid.*, p. 532.

13. *Ibid.*, p. 529.

14. *Ibid.*

15. *Ibid.*, p. 548.

16. *Ibid.*, p. 560.

17. *Ibid.*, p. 549.

18. *Ibid.*, p. 561.

19. *Ibid.*, p. 562.

20. James Daniel and John G. Hubbell, *Strike in the West: The Complete Story of the Cuban Crisis* (New York: Holt, Rinehart and Winston,

1963). For a relatively similar conservative viewpoint, see James E. McSherry, *Khrushchev and Kennedy in Retrospect* (Palo Alto, Calif.: The Open-Door Press, 1971).

21. Daniel and Hubbel, *Strike in the West*, pp. 4, 13.
22. *Ibid.*, p. 20.
23. *Ibid.*, pp. 59–60.
24. *Ibid.*, p. 52.
25. *Ibid.*, pp. 53–54.
26. *Ibid.*, pp. 111–12.
27. *Ibid.*, pp. 47–48.
28. *Ibid.*, p. 56.
29. *Ibid.*, p. 125.
30. *Ibid.*, p. 147.
31. *Ibid.*, p. 155.
32. *Ibid.*, p. 168.
33. *Ibid.*, p. 170.
34. Thomas A. Lane, *The Leadership of President Kennedy* (Caldwell, Idaho: The Caxton Printers, 1964).
35. *Ibid.*, p. 90.
36. *Ibid.*, p. 91.
37. *Ibid.*, p. 90.
38. *Ibid.*, p. 96.
39. *Ibid.*, p. 93.
40. *Ibid.*
41. *Ibid.*, p. 94.
42. *Ibid.*
43. *Ibid.*
44. *Ibid.*, p. 97.
45. *Ibid.*, p. 95.
46. *Ibid.*, p. 96.
47. *Ibid.*, p. 97.
48. Malcolm E. Smith, Jr., *Kennedy's Thirteen Greatest Mistakes in the White House* (New York: The National Forum of America, 1968).
49. *Ibid.*, pp. 134, 136.
50. *Ibid.*, p. 136.
51. *Ibid.*, pp. 127, 131.
52. *Ibid.*, p. 121.
53. *Ibid.*, p. 132.
54. *Ibid.*, p. 136.
55. *Ibid.*, pp. 138–39.
56. *Ibid.*, p. 140.
57. *Ibid.*, p. 235.

58. *Ibid.*, p. 237.

59. *Ibid.*, p. 238.

60. Dean Acheson, "Dean Acheson's Version of Robert Kennedy's Version of the Cuban Missile Affair: Homage to Plain Dumb Luck," *Esquire,* February 1969, pp. 44, 46, 76–77.

61. *Ibid.*, p. 46.

62. *Ibid.*

63. *Ibid.*, p. 76.

64. *Ibid.*

65. *Ibid.*, p. 77.

66. *Ibid.*

67. *Ibid.*, p. 46.

68. *Ibid.*, p. 77.

69. *Ibid.*, pp. 44, 46.

70. *Ibid.*, p. 46.

71. Mario Lazo, *Dagger in the Heart: American Policy Failures in Cuba* (New York: Funk and Wagnalls, 1968).

72. *Ibid.*, p. 330.

73. *Ibid.*, pp. 330–31.

74. *Ibid.*, p. 330.

75. *Ibid.*, p. 324.

76. *Ibid.*, p. 332.

77. *Ibid.*, pp. 332, 348.

78. *Ibid.*, p. 374.

79. *Ibid.*

80. *Ibid.*, pp. 376–77.

81. *Ibid.*, p. 364.

82. *Ibid.*, p. 324.

83. *Ibid.*, p. 400.

84. *Ibid.*, p. 378.

85. Paul D. Bethel, *The Losers: The Definitive Report, by an Eyewitness, of the Communist Conquest of Cuba and the Soviet Penetration in Latin America* (New Rochelle, N.Y.: Arlington House, 1969).

86. *Ibid.*, p. 368.

87. *Ibid.*, p. 337.

88. *Ibid.*, pp. 330, 332.

89. *Ibid.*, pp. 336, 339.

90. *Ibid.*, p. 342.

91. *Ibid.*, p. 344.

92. *Ibid.*, p. 348.

93. *Ibid.*, pp. 347, 349.

94. *Ibid.*, p. 367.

6

THE REVISIONIST INTERPRETATION: THE LEFT-WING PERSPECTIVE

The left-wing interpretation of the Cuban missile crisis represents a perspective that is at variance with both the traditional and the right-wing interpretations. Writing primarily within the decade of the 1970s, the persons advocating this particular revisionist perspective are comprised of journalists, free-lance writers, historians, and political scientists. The basic thrust of this interpretation is that President Kennedy intentionally raised the Cuban episode to the level of crisis and confrontation and thereby unnecessarily, irresponsibly, and recklessly subjected the world to the threat of nuclear holocaust.

The left-wing interpreters accuse the President of rejecting a diplomatic policy via private negotiations for a policy of public confrontation. According to these critics, Kennedy rejected a political solution to what was essentially a political problem, a problem of prestige and appearance, and instituted instead a military response, an act of war.

These revisionists also accuse the President of seeking to satisfy his personal and political needs rather than the security needs of the country. Thus, for the sake of personal prestige and political success, Kennedy adopted a belligerent course so that he could demonstrate his toughness, firmness, and manliness to the world.

The aftermath of the crisis, according to the left-wing perspective, was not victory but rather arrogance. This arrogance led to U.S. confidence in the politics of escalation and in the advantages of seeking military solutions to international political problems; such arrogance led the United States to escalate its action in Vietnam. Furthermore, the Nuclear Test Ban Treaty of 1963, purportedly a by-product of the crisis, did not lead to arms limitation as intended but instead to increased nuclear competition.

As David Lowenthal was preparing the first important right-wing revisionist attack on the traditionalist interpretation of the Cuban missile crisis, Roger Hagan was writing the first significant left-wing revisionist perspective of the U.S.-Soviet nuclear showdown of 1962. Hagan, pacifist and editor of *The Correspondent*, commenced the left-wing counterattack in the 1963 winter issue of *Dissent*.[1] In "Cuba: Triumph or Tragedy?" Hagan contends that President Kennedy rejected a policy of negotiation in favor of a policy of "righteous realpolitik" that only confirmed Khrushchev's belief in the necessity to disperse Soviet weapons to extraterritorial trouble spots, such as Cuba; thus Kennedy's demonstration of resolve had exactly the opposite effect from that intended. The crisis, therefore, was indeed a tragedy, for it served no long-range legal or pacific goals.[2]

According to Hagan, the President was confronted with two alternative risks in his decision-making process: he could follow a belligerent course of action that would involve the risk of war, or he could follow a pacifist policy that would risk his political future and that of the Democratic party. Faced with this dilemma, the President chose the belligerent course and then concocted false reasons to justify his panic reaction.[3]

The central argument in the administration's defense of its response to the so-called crisis, according to Hagan, was that the Soviet missiles in Cuba seriously altered the strategic balance of power and therein represented a military peril to the security of the United States. Hagan claims, however, that the nuclear missiles neither affected the U.S. first-strike capacity nor its retaliatory second-strike capability.[4] In addition to this argument, the administration suggested that its belligerent course was justified because the missiles in Cuba were offensive and the Soviets had deliberately deceived the President in their assurances that offensive weapons would never be deployed in

Cuba. To Hagan, such arguments were only a pretext to justify the President's self-righteous and unilateral course of action. Hagan claims that the question of why Soviet missiles in Cuba could be assumed to be offensive while U.S. missiles in Turkey were assumed to be defensive never surpassed the level of superficial probing. Yet by charging that the missiles in Cuba were offensive, the President could accuse the Soviets of deception.[5] Hence, Hagan states: "Politics, toughness, a sense of nakedness and military peril, a sense of being tested, silly rage, all were probably mingled into an unanalyzed conviction of the necessity of our action."[6]

According to Hagan, it was desirable to have the missiles withdrawn from Cuba, not because they represented a military peril, but because the missiles added to the arms race and could have been a possible cause of accidental war. Nonetheless, the removal of the missiles was the proper aim of negotiation rather than unilateral action. Hagan therefore contends that the Soviet missiles in Cuba "hardly justified sudden unilateral action with any risk of immediate war, particularly action which . . . left the choice . . . to the other side."[7]

The first far-left-wing perspective of the crisis appeared in the 1965 spring issue of *Studies on the Left*, an academic journal of the "new left."[8] In an article entitled "The Cuban Crisis Revisited," Leslie Dewart, professor of philosophy at the University of Toronto, analyzes the Soviet motives for deploying nuclear missiles to Cuba and the U.S. counterscheme to secure their removal.

According to Dewart, the Soviet objective was to force a settlement of the Cuban issue within the broad context of the Cold War. That is, the Soviet Union sought to deter an attack on Cuba while simultaneously compelling the United States to negotiate a settlement of the Berlin problem in favor of the communists. Khrushchev's real objective, therefore, was not strategic but political. Hence, the Soviets did not attempt physical secrecy. On the contrary, they believed that the United States would accept the emplacement of nuclear missiles in Cuba if the missiles were deployed gradually; they wanted the United States to know that the missiles were being sent to Cuba so that the United States would not overreact to a sudden "discovery." The only planned deception by the Soviets was the pretense to the United States that the missiles had been given to the Cubans while, in actuality, they remained under complete control of the Russians. This deception was considered essential if the missiles were to have a credible deterrence effect.[9]

Dewart claims that the U.S. government misled the Soviets into believing that it would accept the emplacement of missiles in Cuba when, in reality, the United States did not intend to do so; the real deceiver in the crisis was the United States and not the Soviet Union. The U.S. counterscheme to the Soviet venture was to pretend surprise at the purported discovery of the missiles in Cuba, and then, with the support of an aroused public, to demand the unconditional removal of the nuclear weapons.[10]

Because Kennedy did not want to negotiate with Khrushchev on the legality of communist Cuba's right to exist, the President believed that deception was the only way to disrupt the Soviet scheme. Thus, according to Dewart, the United States developed the following strategy to thwart Khrushchev's objectives:

(1) Keep the public partly uninformed, partly misinformed about the nature of the Soviet buildup, including the presence of the missiles, and about the nature of the Soviet objectives, (2) convey to the Soviets at the right time the impression that the U.S. reluctantly accepted the Soviet move, (3) issue equivocal statements which would not undeceive the Soviets, but which could later be made to appear to domestic (and world) opinion as a stern warning to the Soviet Union against deployment of the missiles, (4) wait, then, about six weeks until the missiles were emplaced (with the added bonus that this would bring the U.S. to within two weeks of national elections), (5) feign astonishment at the "discovery" of the weapons, (6) obtain the backing of public opinion with the pretense that the missiles gravely endangered U.S. security and upset the strategic balance and with the charge that the Soviets mounted this threat through deception and stealth, and finally (7) demand the unconditional withdrawal of the bombers and missiles.[11]

According to Dewart, the military situation in Cuba was not altered by the withdrawal of the missiles, just as it had not been changed radically by their introduction. What had changed was Kennedy's perspective that it was no longer expedient to overthrow forcibly the Cuban government. Furthermore, the President acquired an awareness that he had not been as clear-sighted as he should have been during the crisis; he alone had placed the entire world in the danger of a thermonuclear holocaust.[12]

The first "new left" criticism of President Kennedy's handling of the missile crisis to appear in a revisionist book was David Horowitz's *The Free World Colossus* (1965).[13] Horowitz, editor of *Ramparts* and former director of research for the Bertrand Russell Peace Foundation, charges Kennedy with intentionally overreacting to the Soviet maneuver in Cuba and, thereby, needlessly threatening the lives and destinies of millions of people throughout the world. From Horowitz's vantage point, the confrontation was unnecessary in that the missiles did not involve a question of strategic balance but rather political balance. What was at stake was not U.S. security and military defense but rather U.S. prestige and appearance. Yet the President seized upon the situation as an opportunity to demonstrate U.S. nuclear superiority and his willingness to risk war.

According to Horowitz, the Soviet missiles in Cuba did not affect the overall nuclear balance despite the false argument that the presence of missiles ninety miles from U.S. shores altered the nuclear status quo. On the contrary, the United States was under no greater military threat from the Soviet Union after the emplacement of missiles in Cuba than it was prior to their introduction. Taken in its totality, the nuclear power of the Soviet Union remained unchanged by the Cuban situation.[14]

What, then, was at stake for the United States by the Soviet emplacement of missiles in Cuba? Horowitz contends that the real stake was the political balance of power that was actually in danger of being changed and that such a change involved a question of prestige and appearance. The Kennedy administration believed that acceptance of a switch in the political balance of world power would be viewed by its critics as appeasement and as a sign that the United States lacked the determination to confront a Soviet challenge.[15] Hence the President and the members of Ex Com agreed that the United States had to demonstrate its strength and compel a Soviet retreat.[16] Now was the time to move against Khrushchev's Cold War offensive. Here was the opportunity for which President Kennedy had been waiting. As Horowitz states:

Having built a sizeable missile superiority of its own, and having laid the plans for a rapid increase in this superiority in the next few years, the Kennedy Administration had waited for an opportune moment to demonstrate its nuclear superiority to the world, and with the prestige thus gained, tip the scales of the world power balance. The test was expected to come in Berlin, when Cuba presented itself.[17]

President Kennedy's desire for personal and national prestige dictated his response to the Soviet venture in Cuba. He spurned the normal diplomatic channels in favor of a naval blockade, an act of war. Rather than present to the Soviet Union an ultimatum in private before the presence of the missiles was disclosed to the world, Kennedy decided to place the prestige of the United States on the line by a public confrontation.[18]

While Kennedy's prestige increased during the crisis by his dispelling any illusion that the United States would not fight for what it considered its vital interests, credit for the resolution of the crisis belongs to Khrushchev. In withdrawing the Soviet missiles from Cuba in the face of U.S. intransigence, Khrushchev demonstrated his moderation and rationality; he alone lifted the threat of nuclear annihilation from the entire world.[19]

According to Horowitz, the President's demonstration of U.S. nuclear superiority in the crisis did not induce the Soviets to acquiesce in this superiority for the future as Kennedy had hoped; rather, it gave impetus to the Soviets to seek their own nuclear superiority. The Cuban missile crisis therefore initiated a new stage in the arms race and an increase in the number of nuclear weapons. As a result of the crisis, the world became a more difficult place to disarm.[20]

"The Brink" (1966), an article in the *New York Review of Books* by I. F. Stone, journalistic critic of U.S. foreign policy, is a scathing indictment of President Kennedy in the world's first thermonuclear confrontation.[21] The nuclear ordeal was nothing less than a game of political prestige between the President and the Premier to see who would back down first. The real question was: "Are you chicken or not?"[22] The real issue was the courage and credibility of John F. Kennedy; that is, was the President prepared to risk nuclear holocaust if the Premier did not withdraw the missiles?[23]

Stone accuses Kennedy of placing his political interests above the safety of the nation. Kennedy knew if the missiles were still in Cuba at the time of the November elections, then the Democrats would suffer a disastrous defeat at the polls. Because the elections were only a couple of weeks away, the President could not afford to wait on prolonged negotiations; he had to repair the political damage done to him and his party before the election.[24] Kennedy therefore rejected the diplomacy of negotiation and sought the unconditional surrender of Khrushchev through nuclear confrontation.[25].

Stone wonders whether Americans, if consulted, would have cared to risk total destruction so that the President could demonstrate his resolve to the world. If Kennedy was concerned about the safety of the United States rather than his own political safety, he may have been willing to sacrifice the Democrats' chances in the election by seeking to negotiate the missile issue.[26] The President never considered the wishes of the American people; he never considered that "given the choice between the danger of a Republican majority in the House and the danger of a thermonuclear war, voters might conceivably have thought the former somewhat less frightening and irreversible."[27]

According to Stone, while Khrushchev shares with Kennedy the responsibility for needlessly bringing the world to the brink of nuclear disaster, the world is indebted to Khrushchev for successfully terminating the confrontation. Unlike the Kennedy brothers, the Chairman fortunately did not prefer his prestige to the prospect of a nuclear world war.[28]

In "Endgame" (1969), an article in *The New York Review of Books*, Ronald Steel reiterates and develops the Stone thesis.[29] Steel, former vice-consul in the U.S. Foreign Service and lecturer at Yale University, contends that President Kennedy rejected traditional methods of diplomacy for a policy of confrontation because he needed a victory in foreign policy on the eve of the 1962 congressional elections. Steel also contends that the administration was lax in its intelligence operations and did not understand the Russian motives for the deployment of missiles to Cuba.

Steel charges that President Kennedy was obsessed with his image and feared that Chairman Khrushchev would never again take his pronouncements seriously if he did not exhibit firmness in the Cuban ordeal. Furthermore, Kennedy knew that to take the Cuban missile issue to the United Nations or to compromise by trading U.S. missiles in Turkey for Soviet missiles in Cuba would be politically unwise just before the elections. Kennedy also believed that if he did not respond courageously in the Cuban situation, then the Russians might be tempted to follow their same policy of adventurism in Central Europe. Hence party politics and foreign policy considerations reinforced Kennedy's decision to demand the complete and unilateral withdrawal of the missiles before the end of October; it was a demand premised on the public humiliation of the Kremlin.[30]

Steel claims that the Kennedy administration was caught by surprise by the covert introduction of Soviet missiles into Cuba, but it should not have been so. The administration's skepticism about Republican charges of such activity combined with Kennedy's reluctance to face a Cuban crisis on the eve of the congressional elections led to the failure of the administration to draw proper conclusions from its intelligence evidence.[31]

Steel also claims that the President's concern about the Berlin issue led him to misread the Soviet motives. According to Steel, the President believed that the Cuban missile maneuver was an attempt by the Soviets to force the U.S. allies out of Berlin in exchange for the withdrawal of the missiles in the Western Hemisphere. Thus the administration failed to understand the real Soviet motives, which were: (1) to redress the strategic imbalance, (2) to protect Castro's communism, and (3) to strengthen the Soviet position in the Caribbean and in Latin America.[32]

Despite the President's initiating a public confrontation, Steel gives Kennedy credit for overcoming the hawks in his administration. Yet he believes that Kennedy was lucky that Khrushchev decided to withdraw the missiles rather than make Cuba a test of personal and national virility. Steel concludes that the American-Soviet confrontation demonstrated "how the fate of mankind rests in the hands of a few individuals driven by perfectly ordinary fears, anxieties, and rivalries. The Cuban missile crisis was a very close call, and it could have gone the other way."[33]

By the 1970s, the left-wing perspective even became included in edited documentaries of the crisis. Robert Beggs, editor of *The Cuban Missile Crisis* (1971), included a commentary in which he analyzed the crisis as an event having developed over the issue of prestige; Khrushchev emplaced the missiles in Cuba for the sake of personal prestige while Kennedy demanded their removal for the same objective.[34]

Beggs discounts the postcrisis theories that the Soviet motivation in establishing missiles in Cuba was either to deter a U.S. attack and secure a U.S. pledge against invasion or to obtain the removal of missiles in Turkey. The emplacement of missiles in Cuba was an attempt "to reinforce socialism on an international scale."[35] Russia sought to improve immensely its prestige in the world and its bargaining power in Europe.[36]

As Khrushchev attempted to emplace missiles in Cuba for the sake of prestige, so Kennedy attempted to get them removed for the sake of prestige.[37] Failure to confront Russia would indicate that the United States would not risk anything to challenge Russia. Yet Kennedy acted not only in the name of U.S. prestige but for the sake of personal prestige. "If Kennedy had delayed and faced the elections with the Soviet missiles fully installed in Cuba, it would have spelt political disaster for the Administration."[38] Immediate action, therefore, was absolutely necessary from Kennedy's perspective, but the risks inherent in the administration's blockade were appalling.[39]

In *Cold War and Counterrevolution* (1972), "new left" historian Richard J. Walton, former United Nations correspondent and lecturer in international relations, presents President Kennedy as the great counterrevolutionary of the post-World War II era.[40] Driven by his machismo character, by his concern for the 1962 elections, and by his need for personal prestige, President Ken-

nedy unnecessarily, irresponsibly, and recklessly took the world
to the brink of nuclear war. Without sufficient reason, Kennedy consciously risked thermonuclear catastrophe.[41] Thus the
President's behavior during the crisis was "irresponsible and
reckless to a supreme degree. . . ."[42]

Walton claims that the President, by his unrelenting hostility
to Cuba, caused the development of the confrontation in the
first place.[43] Khrushchev had every right to emplace missiles in
Cuba. Had it not been for the Bay of Pigs fiasco, the Soviet
Union would not have had cause to put Soviet defensive missiles in Cuba. While Kennedy referred to these missiles as offensive, they did not differ from the Jupiter missiles in Turkey,
which were considered defensive.[44] The Soviet Union only followed the policy of the United States when the latter emplaced
missiles in Turkey. Both were intended to deter aggressive acts.[45]

Khrushchev perhaps may have been reckless and foolish in
putting missiles in Cuba; he may have made a serious and dangerous miscalculation. But Kennedy did not have to exploit the
situation.[46] Kennedy took a U.S.-Cuban issue and made it a
test of American determination with the Soviet Union; he made
it a crucial episode in the Cold War.[47]

While Khrushchev was justified by international law in
transporting missiles to Cuba, he was not justified by common
sense. The Chairman could have secured protection of Cuba
by less extreme means, such as by a foreign policy declaration.
Because of U.S. political realities, however, Kennedy felt compelled to act. Yet he was not forced to act recklessly; he could
have followed a less reckless course through diplomacy.[48] Instead, Kennedy followed the path of demanding "unconditional surrender with all its unforeseeable consequences."[49]
Despite arguments to the contrary, Kennedy gave Khrushchev
only two options: humiliating retreat or nuclear war.[50]

According to Walton, President Kennedy may never have
considered that Khrushchev might believe that Russia had a
legal right to deploy missiles to Cuba and that the U.S. act of
war, the blockade, could have triggered a Soviet military response. Nonetheless, Kennedy sought an unconditional and
public surrender from a proud adversary who might well have
believed he was in the right and the President in the wrong.[51]

While many believe that Kennedy secured a great personal victory in outbluffing Khrushchev, the Premier obtained all that he sought originally in his decision to emplace missiles in Cuba— namely, a guarantee of Cuban security and the removal of U.S. missiles in Turkey and Italy.[52] Most of all, Khrushchev did successfully terminate the crisis by accepting humiliation rather than war, but Walton wonders whether "Kennedy would have been able to accept public humiliation as the cost of avoiding nuclear war."[53] While Walton wonders, he emphatically believes not.

The thesis initiated by Stone, perpetuated by Steel, and expanded by Walton is continued in *The Kennedy Doctrine* (1972) by Louise FitzSimons, a former foreign affairs officer for the Atomic Energy Commission and research publications editor at the Carnegie Endowment for International Peace.[54] The doctrine is based on Kennedy's belief, as a Cold War warrior, that the United States could and should affect decisively the course of events around the globe. Therefore, once Kennedy decided that Cuba was a primary concern of U.S. foreign policy then there were no limits to U.S. action or reaction to events in Cuba.

FitzSimons accuses President Kennedy of misinterpreting the Soviet motives for emplacing missiles in Cuba. Kennedy believed that the purportedly covert introduction of missiles in Cuba was part of a Soviet scheme in Cold War politics to undermine U.S. credibility in Europe and Latin America. To the President and most of the members of Ex Com, any alteration in the political balance of power was totally unacceptable.[55] Yet the primary motive of the Soviets was to attempt to redress the strategic imbalance of nulcear power; it was an attempt to eliminate partially what the Soviets considered to be an intolerable threat, a threat posed by the U.S. preponderance of nuclear weapons that could eliminate the Soviet Union's retaliatory nuclear capacity. Kennedy's concern with prestige and credibility, however, prevented him from understanding the real motive behind the Soviet emplacement of missiles in Cuba.[56]

FitzSimons charges the President with raising the Soviet-Cuban incident arbitrarily to the level of a crisis by his public confrontation with Khrushchev via Kennedy's worldwide broadcast of October 22.[57] If the missiles in Cuba represented only a political rather than a strategic alteration of the balance of power, as the President so believed, then why did Kennedy confront Khrushchev with a naval blockade and the threat of further action? What necessitated the rapid removal of the missiles and the rejection of a policy of private negotiations?

According to FitzSimons, the President rejected private diplomacy because such might be considered appeasement, and he might appear weak to Khrushchev, but he accepted the course of public confrontation so that he could convey the false impression that a dire threat to U.S. national existence had suddenly arisen. Such an announcement, Kennedy believed, would assure him of widespread public support for his demand that the Soviets immediately and unconditionally withdraw their missiles from Cuba; it also would provide him with support to take whatever further action he might deem necessary.[58] Why the need for such hurry? Kennedy believed that unless the missiles were removed before the November elections the American people would elect a Republican House of Representatives.[59] According to FitzSimons,

considerations of strategy—political if not military—convinced the President that the Russian withdrawal would have to be complete; considerations of prestige convinced him that it would have to be unilateral; and considerations of partisan politics convinced him that the withdrawal would have to be brought about by the end of October.[60]

FitzSimons believes that the only time a President has a right to risk a thermonuclear holocaust is in the face of national extinction. Such a prospect did not exist for Kennedy by the Soviet deployment of missiles of Cuba. Yet the President raised the incident to a crisis by his rhetoric and thereby brought the world to the brink of nuclear destruction. Kennedy acted as he did because: (1) he feared that his prestige would suffer; (2) he feared that Khrushchev would think he lacked determination and firmness; and (3) he feared that the American public would remove his party or even himself from office.[61]

The Kennedy Neurosis (1973) by Nancy Gager Clinch, a freelance writer, is a psychohistory of the Kennedy brothers.[62] According to Clinch, the Kennedys sought power to satisfy their own inner needs rather than to fulfill a desire to serve their fellowmen. John Kennedy, even as President, doubted his own worth as an individual, and he constantly needed to compete and to prove his courage. Thus, from a sense of powerlessness and rejection, Kennedy developed an obsessive and compulsive need for power and social recognition.[63] This neurosis developed not only out of the Kennedy family history but also out of the nation's neurosis: its compulsive drive for material success, its belief in its own omnipotence, and its sense of crusading mission to spread the blessings of the United States throughout the world.[64]

According to Clinch, the Soviet missiles in Cuba presented a challenge to Kennedy's prestige both as the leader and defender of Latin America and as the leader of the Democratic party, which most certainly would have lost the November elections if the missiles were not withdrawn before election day. Since the missiles did not alter the balance of strategic nuclear power, Kennedy took the challenge as a personal one.[65] But his response to the Soviet maneuver in Cuba "brought the United States perilously near to a nuclear holocaust without rational need."[66]

President Kennedy, Clinch contends, rejected the possibility of following a diplomatic course of action in the missile crisis because he needed to demonstrate his competitiveness and his courage; he needed to show that he was not too soft to fight and that he could confront an adversary. Thus Kennedy decided to force Khrushchev into a public confrontation, a public showdown. This decision of the President was dictated by his emotional needs rather than by the security needs of his country.[67]

According to Clinch, two specific incidents in the missile crisis support the contention that President Kennedy's unconscious emotional needs and conscious political needs took precedence over the safety of the nation. The first incident was Kennedy's refusal to exchange U.S. missiles in Turkey for Soviet missiles in Cuba, even though the missiles in Turkey were obsolete and militarily worthless. Yet Kennedy refused the exchange, for he feared that his image might be tarnished by critics calling such action a surrender; his personal needs demanded a Russian surrender, not a U.S. compromise on an exchange of missiles.[68]

The second incident that Clinch cites is the extremely limited time period for Soviet acquiescence that Robert Kennedy conveyed to Ambassador Dobrynin on Saturday evening, October 27. It was at this meeting that the Attorney General suggested to the Ambassador that time was extremely short and unless the Soviets removed their missiles immediately, the United States would take strong retaliatory action. Such action, Clinch claims, could mean nothing other than an attack on the missile sites and an invasion of Cuba. Hence, at the height of the crisis, the Kennedy brothers directly challenged Khrushchev with the possibility of World War III.[69]

Clinch believes that the President was prepared to initiate a nuclear war over Cuba; Khrushchev was not. The Chairman capitulated and suffered humiliation for the sake of Kennedy's prestige and world peace.[70] Thus Clinch concludes: "Fortunately for us all, Khrushchev was not so imbued with the neuroticism of Kennedy's machismo, and suffered humiliation rather than wreak destruction."[71]

The Kennedy Promise (1973) is a revisionist account of the Kennedy presidency by Henry Fairlie, a British journalist.[72] Fairlie's thesis is that Kennedy's politics repeatedly followed a progression: the politics of expectation, the politics of crisis, and the politics of confrontation. The President aroused the American people to a high expectation of what politics could accomplish. Under the stress of high expectations, problems became magnified into crises; then, under the additional stress of a crisis atmosphere, the President sought solutions in confrontation. What Kennedy did for a thousand days, the American people did for the entire decade of the 1960s.[73]

Like Walton and FitzSimons, Fairlie views Kennedy as a Cold War warrior after the Cold War was over. Kennedy was not so much concerned with the Russian empire as he was with Soviet communism; he was not so much concerned with the Chinese empire as he was with communist China. Thus he lacked an understanding of world politics and concentrated on ideology.[74]

Kennedy also lacked an understanding of power. Power, according to Fairlie, generates opportunities over a period of time. Kennedy, however, considered power only in terms of immediate strength, not in terms of its duration. Kennedy therefore governed by crisis as an instrument of policy. Every policy was subjected to crisis, and every crisis was used in turn to stimulate people to respond in accordance with the wishes of the administration. According to Fairlie, Kennedy was only following his belief, expressed in *Profiles in Courage*, that great crises produce great men.[75]

Fairlie contends that the politics of crisis and confrontation exercised by President Kennedy during the Cuban missile crisis were an irresponsible use of power. It was only by fortune and plain dumb luck that Kennedy's crisis politics in this case did not lead to the incineration of the world. What is most frightening, however, is that if Khrushchev had not backed down, the President was prepared to take the ultimate step; he was prepared for thermonuclear war.[76]

Because the American people had become attuned to the politics of crisis, they did not question the President when he informed them that a crisis existed. Yet, by generating an atmosphere of crisis and displaying spectacular personal leadership, he exaggerated in the public mind the military power of the United States and its ability to use the power.[77]

Fairlie concludes that the Kennedy legacy is that he had accustomed the people of the United States to live in a crisis atmosphere and to seek solutions to crises in confrontations. Because of his politics, the world from which Kennedy departed was far more threatening to the United States than it was when he assumed the presidency.[78]

"The Cuban Missile Crisis" (1974) by Barton J. Bernstein, "new left" historian at Stanford University, is another scathing indictment of Kennedy and his response to the emplacement of Soviet missiles in Cuba.[79] In his essay, published in Lynn Miller and Ronald Pruessen's *Reflections on the Cold War*, Bernstein contends that politics and prestige influenced Kennedy inordinately, and this influence caused the President to take more extreme action than the situation warranted.

Bernstein dismisses the argument that the missiles were emplaced clandestinely in Cuba by emphasizing that they were not camouflaged. He then castigates Kennedy for using arbitrary and self-righteous definitions to classify the missiles in Cuba as offensive.[80] According to Bernstein, the President's definitions did not rely on the nature of the weapons but on his administration's assumptions about the intention of the possessor.[81]

While Khrushchev put nuclear missiles in Cuba as an attempt to placate the Chinese Maoists who considered Soviet foreign policy too unaggressive, to satisfy the Russian militarists who demanded increased military preparedness, and to support a revolutionary communist regime in the Western Hemisphere, the missiles did not alter the strategic balance of power, according to Bernstein. The missiles neither gave the Soviets a first-strike capacity nor did they increase the Soviet capacity for a retaliatory second strike.[82] "Put bluntly, a Soviet first strike was equally implausible with or without the additional missiles—unless the Soviets were suicidal."[83]

Why did Kennedy dismiss the use of private negotiations and implement a public confrontation? According to Bernstein, privately conducted negotiations would have been the appropriate response to the situation. While conceding that private diplomatic maneuvers may have resulted in a brief blow to U.S. prestige and in a temporary loss of initiative, as Kennedy rightfully believed, the negotiations would have given the Soviets more time to consider calmly a response. Such a maneuver would have lessened the possibility of the Soviets acting precipitously, and the probability of nuclear annihilation would have been decreased.[84]

Bernstein sees both a paradoxical and an ironical situation in the Cuban missile crisis. "The paradox . . . is that a nation may go to war in order to maintain the very credibility which is being protected in order to avoid war."[85] The irony of the crisis is that it contributed to a dual and contradictory legacy, "the cooling of passions in Soviet-American relations and an escalation of the arms race."[86]

Jim F. Heath, a disciple of Bernstein and a professor of history at Portland State University, contends in his *Decade of Disillusionment* (1975) that the 1960s began with Americans full of tremendous hope and great expectations and ended with Americans losing faith in their political system as the credibility gap widened.[87] The Cuban crisis contributed to this lack of credibility, especially among U.S. allies. Although Kennedy feared a loss of prestige and credibility among U.S. allies if he did not compel the Soviets to remove the missiles from Cuba, the opposite situation resulted. "Rather than strengthening America's global alliances, the handling of the crisis actually weakened NATO."[88]

Heath agrees with the Kennedy critics that the President placed too much emphasis on prestige and that he went too near the precipice of nuclear war, but he does give credit to Kennedy for not succumbing to the dictates of his advisers: "JFK deserves more credit than he often received for repeatedly . . . opting for a more moderate, less adventurous course in foreign affairs than that recommended by the hawkish cold warriors among his advisors."[89]

In the revisionist tradition of Horowitz, Walton, and Fitz-Simons, political scientist Bruce Miroff of the University of Texas analyzes the Kennedy presidency in *Pragmatic Illusions* (1976).[90] Miroff's central argument about the New Frontier's foreign policy is that President Kennedy spurred the declining Cold War to new explosive heights. By investing local events with decisive global importance, by choosing confrontation to precede diplomacy, and by acting as if he were a lonely leader grappling with the terror of nuclear destruction, Kennedy needlessly made crisis a mark of his administration. As President, Kennedy consistently transformed local affairs into international Cold War crises between the United States and the Soviet Union, and each crisis became a test of U.S. will and resolve.[91]

According to Miroff, Premier Khrushchev emplaced the Soviet missiles in Cuba primarily to restore in some measure the strategic, nuclear equilibrium. In doing so, the Soviets adopted the same tactic that the United States employed five years earlier when it emplaced American intermediate-range ballistic missiles in Turkey, Italy, and England.[92]

While the Soviet strategic scheme was understandable, Miroff concedes that it was a reckless maneuver. It was reckless not only because it was executed clandestinely and deceptively but also because it touched upon the President's most sensitive spot. In the 1960 campaign, Kennedy had criticized the Republicans for their failure to prevent the spread of communism to the Western Hemisphere. Yet when Kennedy became President he failed to dislodge communism from Cuba with the ill-fated Bay of Pigs invasion. He then was stigmatized as a loser and became vulnerable to U.S. criticism on the subject of Cuba. The Soviet action in Cuba, therefore, was not inherently reckless, but it was reckless in view of the fact that John F. Kennedy was President at the time the episode transpired.[93]

President Kennedy did not consider the Russian deployment of missiles to Cuba as a military threat to U.S. security, according to Miroff. Rather, Kennedy believed that the emplacement of missiles in Cuba represented a Soviet gamble for a political Cold War victory; that is, it represented a probe of U.S. determination and resolve. Kennedy thus believed that if the United States did not respond with firmness, then it would appear impotent; its allies would lose faith in its commitments. Yet, despite Kennedy's conviction that the Soviets sought only a political victory in Cuba, Ex Com never considered whether the United States should take military action but considered only what kind of military action was appropriate. As in most foreign policy situations, therefore, Kennedy immediately proceeded to confront rather than to negotiate.[94]

Miroff contends that the blockade was a dangerous response. It was an act of war that established a direct naval confrontation between Soviet and U.S. vessels. It also provided for the rapid movement to more drastic measures. The blockade, in short, provided the means for a nuclear showdown between the United States and the Soviet Union for the sake of personal and national prestige.[95]

Miroff suggests that Kennedy, for the sake of prestige, may have wanted a showdown. Psychologically, the President needed to demonstrate his toughness; politically, he needed a Cold War triumph. These motives, then, compelled the President to reject a negotiated exchange of the U.S. missiles in Turkey for the Soviet missiles in Cuba. For the sake of these same motives, the President suggested that the United States would take further military action if the Soviets did not drop their proposal for an exchange of these bases. Hence, at the height of the crisis, Kennedy was prepared to carry the confrontation to its climax—nuclear catastrophe.[96]

Miroff summarizes his interpretation of the crisis thusly:

Eschewing a diplomatic approach, insisting upon the use of force to compel a Russian retreat, Kennedy had brought the world to the brink of nuclear war for the sake of American prestige and influence. At the height of the crisis, he abdicated control over the outbreak of hostilities to Khrushchev's sense of restraint. . . . Kennedy's conduct in the missile crisis was neither responsible nor justifiable.[97]

What were the ultimate results of the crisis? According to Miroff, there were two negative results. First, with renewed arrogance from the Cuban missile triumph, the United States set out in Vietnam to reproduce successfully its victorious politics of escalation and confrontation. Second, the United States signed a test ban treaty ostensibly to limit the arms race but which, in actuality, only established a new stage in the nuclear competition.[98]

Perhaps the left-wing perspective is best summarized in Thomas G. Paterson's *Virginia Quarterly Review* article, "Bearing the Burden" (1978).[99] Paterson, professor of history at the University of Connecticut, views Kennedy and the members of his administration as part of the containment generation, that generation which believed that toughness contains communism, that a nation must avoid compromises, that communism is monolithic, and that a powerful United States alone has the duty to protect a threatened world. This Cold War ideology, when combined with the action-oriented style of the Kennedy administration, produced a belligerent foreign policy, one of crises and confrontations.[100]

Paterson believes that President Kennedy was driven by a psychological desire for power, for power ensured winning. It was not acceptable just to try; acceptance came only with winning. Hence Kennedy was eager to prove his toughness, to prove he was a winner. Within this psychic framework, therefore, Kennedy personalized issues and converted them into tests of will. Politics, especially foreign affairs, became a matter of crises and races.[101]

The Cuban missile crisis presented a unique opportunity to Kennedy to demonstrate his toughness, according to Paterson. The crisis provided the President with an opportunity to demonstrate his manliness and to exercise his management skills. It also gave him the opportunity to release his revenge for the disastrous Bay of Pigs. These needs dictated the President's response to the emplacement of Soviet missiles in Cuba.[102] For the sake of toughness, manliness, and revenge, the President rejected diplomacy, even private diplomacy, in favor of a public confrontation via a television address, even though such action significantly increased the chances of war.[103]

The President's desire to score a victory, to recapture previous losses, and to flex his muscles accentuated the crisis and obstructed diplomacy. . . . Kennedy gave Khrushchev no chance to withdraw his mistake or to save face. . . . He left little room for bargaining but instead issued a public ultimatum and seemed willing to destroy, in Strangelovian fashion, millions in the process.[104]

Like Miroff, Paterson presents some negative results stemming from the missile crisis. First, following its public humiliation and recognizing its nuclear inferiority, the Soviet Union launched a massive arms buildup. Second, following its triumph in the crisis, the United States enshrined force as an instrument of policy and sought military solutions to political problems. Finally, the victory in Cuba encouraged the Kennedy administration, later the Johnson administration, to take firmer action in Vietnam.[105]

While the criticisms of the interpreters of the left-wing perspective of the Cuban missile crisis range from the restrained to the highly critical, the writers do form a cohesive interpretation. The liberals represented in this perspective generally agree that the emplacement of Soviet missiles in Cuba in October 1962 did not alter the strategic balance of nuclear power in the world but only the political balance (Dewart, Horowitz, Clinch, Bernstein, Miroff); that is, the missiles did not represent a military threat to the security of the United States (Hagan, Dewart, Horowitz, Stone, Steel, Clinch, Bernstein, Miroff). Yet President Kennedy overreacted, as if a threat existed, by raising the incident to the level of a crisis and thereby, without rational need, irresponsibly and recklessly threatened the lives and destinies of millions of people throughout the world with thermonuclear war (Hagan, Dewart, Horowitz, Stone, Steel, Beggs, Walton, FitzSimons, Clinch, Fairlie, Bernstein, Heath, Miroff, Paterson).

As to the motive behind the Soviet decision to deploy missiles in Cuba, the left-wing interpreters are divided. Several believe that the motive was to protect Cuba from a U.S. invasion; the missiles were emplaced in Cuba for purely defensive purposes (Dewart, Steel, Walton). Other motives to which the interpreters give credence are: (1) to redress in appearance the strategic nuclear imbalance (Steel, FitzSimons, Miroff); (2) to reinforce socialism on an international scale, especially in the Western Hemisphere (Steel, Beggs, Bernstein); (3) to reinforce the Soviet bargaining position on Berlin (Dewart, Beggs); and (4) to placate the Maoists and the Russian militarists (Bernstein). Whatever the motive, however, Khrushchev was justified in emplacing missiles in Cuba by international law but not by common sense (Walton). It was a reckless move not only because it was executed clandestinely and deceptively but also primarily because it was an affront to the ever-sensitive John F. Kennedy, Cold War warrior (Miroff).

The President initially and later Ex Com arbitrarily and superficially made a distinction between the Soviet "offensive" missiles in Cuba and the U.S. "defensive" missiles in Turkey when in fact both were emplaced in allied countries for defensive purposes (Hagan, Walton, Bernstein). This distinction permitted Kennedy to accuse the Soviets of deception (Hagan) and to treat the incident as a military rather than a political matter (Miroff).

Using the pretext that the missiles were offensive and thus a threat to U.S. security, the President arbitrarily raised the incident to the level of a crisis and then publicly confronted Chairman Khrushchev with an ultimatum—demanding unconditional surrender (Hagan, Horowitz, Stone, Steel, Beggs, Walton, FitzSimons, Clinch, Fairlie, Miroff, Paterson). Without rational

cause, Kennedy rejected traditional diplomacy via private negotiations (Hagan, Horowitz, Stone, Steel, Beggs, Walton,
FitzSimons, Clinch, Fairlie, Miroff, Paterson) and instituted a
naval blockade, an act of war, against the Soviet Union (Horowitz, Walton, Miroff); it was a unilateral act of "self-righteous realpolitik" (Hagan).

The President rejected diplomacy and initiated a confrontation because he feared a negotiated settlement would mean appeasement (Horowitz, FitzSimons). Such would tarnish gravely
his personal prestige and his party's political prestige (Hagan,
Dewart, Stone, Steel, Beggs, Walton, FitzSimons, Clinch, Fairlie, Bernstein, Heath, Miroff, Paterson). Therefore, Kennedy
commenced his response to the Soviet maneuver in Cuba with
a public confrontation so as to secure the support of the American people (Dewart, FitzSimons, Fairlie).

According to the left-wing interpreters, the President viewed
the Soviet deployment of missiles in Cuba as a personal challenge to his prestige, and thus he converted an issue in foreign
affairs to a personal issue, an issue involving his courage to
demonstrate his resolve, toughness, and, given his machismo
character, manliness (Horowitz, Stone, Steel, Walton, Fitz-
Simons, Clinch, Fairlie, Bernstein, Miroff, Paterson). Hence for
the sake of personal prestige, John F. Kennedy was prepared
to risk a thermonuclear showdown, a nuclear catastrophe (Horowitz, Stone, FitzSimons, Clinch, Fairlie, Miroff, Paterson).

Not only did personal, psychological needs dictate the President's response to the emplacement of Soviet missiles in Cuba,
but political considerations also affected his decision. Kennedy
needed a foreign policy "victory" if his Democratic party were
to be successful in the 1962 congressional elections. This political consideration dictated the need to have the missiles withdrawn before the end of October (Hagan, Stone, Steel, Beggs,
Walton, FitzSimons, Clinch, Bernstein). This factor required the
President to act immediately and decisively; it dictated the options that Kennedy presented to Khrushchev: humiliating retreat or nuclear war (Walton, Clinch). Thus the President placed
his political interests and those of the Democratic party above
the safety of the nation (Stone).

While the left-wing interpreters accuse President Kennedy of

initiating the confrontation and threatening the world with nuclear holocaust, they credit Chairman Khrushchev with successfully terminating the crisis. Unlike the President, Khrushchev willingly accepted humiliation as a viable option to the
thermonuclear annihilation of mankind (Horowitz, Stone, Walton, Clinch, Fairlie).

The left-wing perspective of the Cuban missile crisis presents
the ultimate results of the U.S.-Soviet confrontation as purely
negative. The crisis unfortunately served no long-range pacific
or legal goals (Hagan), but rather it served only as an impetus
for a new nuclear arms race (Horowitz, Bernstein, Miroff, Paterson). The unilateral action of the United States led to a loss
of credibility among its allies and weakened NATO (Heath). As
a result of the crisis, the United States gained a renewed confidence in its military power and in its politics of escalation,
which soon turned into arrogance; this arrogance, then, led the
United States to escalate its action in Vietnam (Miroff, Paterson). Finally, the so-called Kennedy triumph in the confrontation led the American people to seek military solutions to purely
international political problems (Fairlie, Paterson).

NOTES

1. Roger Hagan, "Cuba: Triumph or Tragedy?" *Dissent* 10 (Winter
1963): 13–26.

2. *Ibid.*, pp. 25–26.

3. *Ibid.*, pp. 15–17.

4. *Ibid.*, pp. 15, 19. Hagan and Bart Bernstein counter the contention of some strategic analysts that the defense of the United States
depended upon a combination of SAC bombers, which were suscep-
tible to the MRBMs in Cuba, and the Ballistic Missile Early Warning
System, which was aimed northward and could not spot a missile
attack from Cuba. According to Hagan and Bernstein, the combination
of ICBMs (range 2,000–9,000 miles) in the Soviet Union and IRBMs
(range 700–2,000 miles) in Cuba was insufficient to make a first strike
or retaliatory strike feasible against the United States. To support their
contention, Hagan and Bernstein cite the comparative estimates of
strategic strength early in 1963 as compiled by the Institute for Strategic Studies of London: Western Alliances—500 ICBMs and 250
MRBMs; Communist Bloc—75 ICBMs and 700 MRBMs. The United

States also had 630 long-range bombers with a range of over 5,000 miles compared to only 200 for the Soviet Union. Roger Hagan and Bart Bernstein, "Military Value of the Missiles in Cuba," *Bulletin of the Atomic Scientists* 19 (February 1963): 8–13.

5. Hagan, "Cuba," pp. 15–17.

6. *Ibid.*, p. 17.

7. *Ibid.*, p. 19.

8. Leslie Dewart, "The Cuban Crisis Revisited," *Studies on the Left* 5 (Spring 1965): 15–40.

9. *Ibid.*, pp. 19–24.

10. *Ibid.*, p. 24.

11. *Ibid.*, pp. 24–25.

12. *Ibid.*, p. 39.

13. David Horowitz, *The Free World Colossus: A Critique of American Foreign Policy in the Cold War* (New York: Hill and Wang, 1965).

14. *Ibid.*, pp. 383–85.

15. *Ibid.*, p. 386.

16. *Ibid.*, p. 391.

17. *Ibid.*, p. 390.

18. *Ibid.*, pp. 383, 387.

19. *Ibid.*, p. 392.

20. *Ibid.*, pp. 396–97.

21. I. F. Stone, "The Brink," review of *The Missile Crisis* by Elie Abel, in *The New York Review of Books* 6 (April 14, 1966): 12–16; reprinted as "What if Khrushchev Hadn't Backed Down?" in I. F. Stone, *In A Time of Torment* (New York: Random House, 1967).

22. Stone, "The Brink," p. 12.

23. *Ibid.*, p. 13.

24. *Ibid.*

25. *Ibid.*, pp. 13–14.

26. *Ibid.*

27. *Ibid.*, p. 14.

28. *Ibid.*, pp. 15–16.

29. Ronald Steel, "Endgame," review of *Thirteen Days* by Robert F. Kennedy, in *The New York Review of Books* 12 (March 13, 1969): 15–22; reprinted in Ronald Steel, *Imperialists and Other Heroes: A Chronicle of the American Empire* (New York: Random House, 1971). See also Roger Hilsman and Ronald Steel, "An Exchange on the Missile Crisis," *The New York Review of Books* 12 (May 8, 1969): 36–38.

30. Steel, "Endgame," pp. 16–18. John Kenneth Galbraith supports this view, for "once they [the missiles] were there, the political needs of the Kennedy administration urged it to take almost any risk

to get them out." John Kenneth Galbraith, "Storm Over Havana: Who Were the Real Heroes?" *Chicago Tribune*, January 29, 1969, sec. 4, pp. 1, 16.

31. Steel, "Endgame," pp. 19, 20.
32. *Ibid.*, p. 20.
33. *Ibid.*, p. 22.
34. Robert Beggs, ed., *The Cuban Missile Crisis* (London: Longman Group Limited, 1971).
35. *Ibid.*, p. 91.
36. *Ibid.*
37. *Ibid.*
38. *Ibid.*, p. 92.
39. *Ibid.*
40. Richard J. Walton, *Cold War and Counterrevolution: The Foreign Policy of John F. Kennedy* (New York: The Viking Press, 1972).
41. *Ibid.*, pp. 103–04.
42. *Ibid.*, p. 103.
43. *Ibid.*, p. 112.
44. *Ibid.*, pp. 107–17.
45. *Ibid.*, p. 127.
46. *Ibid.*, pp. 116, 122.
47. *Ibid.*, p. 115.
48. *Ibid.*, p. 141.
49. *Ibid.*, p. 128.
50. *Ibid.*, p. 126.
51. *Ibid.*, p. 127.
52. *Ibid.*, pp. 141–42.
53. *Ibid.*, p. 141.
54. Louise FitzSimons, *The Kennedy Doctrine* (New York: Random House, 1972).
55. *Ibid.*, pp. 146, 151–53.
56. *Ibid.*, pp. 146, 148.
57. *Ibid.*, p. 158.
58. *Ibid.*, pp. 160–61.
59. *Ibid.*, p. 155.
60. *Ibid.*, pp. 161–62.
61. *Ibid.*, pp. 169, 172.
62. Nancy Gager Clinch, *The Kennedy Neurosis* (New York: Grosset and Dunlap, 1973).
63. *Ibid.*, p. 19.
64. *Ibid.*, p. 158.
65. *Ibid.*, p. 199.

66. *Ibid.*, p. 198. Sidney Lens supports this view, but he goes even further to state: "The willingness to gamble with the idea of nuclear war, even when victory would simply mean ashes, indicates a loss of touch with reality, almost a suicidal impulse." Sidney Lens, *The Military-Industrial Complex* (Kansas City: Pilgrim Press, 1970), p. 91.

67. Clinch, *Kennedy Neurosis*, pp. 200, 205.

68. *Ibid.*, pp. 202–203.

69. *Ibid.*, pp. 203–204.

70. *Ibid.*, pp. 204–205.

71. *Ibid.*, p. 206.

72. Henry Fairlie, *The Kennedy Promise: The Politics of Expectation* (Garden City, N.Y.: Doubleday, 1973).

73. *Ibid.*, p. 14.

74. *Ibid.*, pp. 297–98.

75. *Ibid.*, pp. 295–308.

76. *Ibid.*, p. 311.

77. *Ibid.*, pp. 313–16.

78. *Ibid.*, p. 316.

79. Barton J. Bernstein, "The Cuban Missile Crisis," in *Reflections on the Cold War: A Quarter Century of American Foreign Policy*, eds. Lynn H. Miller and Ronald W. Pruessen (Philadelphia: Temple University Press, 1974), pp. 108–42. See also by the same author, "Courage and Commitment: The Missiles of October, *Foreign Service Journal* 52 (December 1975): 9–11, 24–27.

80. Bernstein, "The Cuban Missile Crisis," p. 114.

81. *Ibid.*

82. *Ibid.*, pp. 121–25.

83. *Ibid.*, p. 123.

84. *Ibid.*, p. 130.

85. *Ibid.*, p. 134.

86. *Ibid.*, p. 135.

87. Jim F. Heath, *Decade of Disillusionment: The Kennedy-Johnson Years* (Bloomington: Indiana University Press, 1975).

88. *Ibid.*, p. 132.

89. *Ibid.*, p. 133. For a similar assessment of this viewpoint, see George Kateb, "Kennedy as Statesman," *Commentary* 41 (June 1986): 54–60.

90. Bruce Miroff, *Pragmatic Illusions: The Presidential Politics of John F. Kennedy* (New York: David McKay, 1976).

91. *Ibid.*, pp. 65–66, 81, 271.

92. *Ibid.*, pp. 85–86.

93. *Ibid.*, p. 86.

94. *Ibid.*, pp. 88–90.

95. *Ibid.*, pp. 92–94.

96. *Ibid.*, pp. 94–98.

97. *Ibid.*, p. 99.

98. *Ibid.*, pp. 100–09.

99. Thomas G. Paterson, "Bearing the Burden: A Critical Look at JFK's Foreign Policy," *The Virginia Quarterly Review* 54 (Spring 1978): 193–212.

100. *Ibid.*, pp. 193–201.

101. *Ibid.*, p. 202.

102. *Ibid.*, pp. 204–05.

103. *Ibid.*, p. 204.

104. *Ibid.*, p. 206.

105. *Ibid.*, p. 207. For a similar assessment of this viewpoint, see James A. Nathan, "The Missile Crisis: His Finest Hour Now," *World Politics* 27 (January 1975): 265–81.

7

THE STRUCTURALIST INTERPRETATION: THE SOVIETOLOGISTS' PERSPECTIVE

Unlike the interpreters in the previous perspectives, the structuralists are not concerned with praising or condemning the President for his actions or lack thereof during the Cuban missile crisis. The structuralists are concerned primarily with the motive and/or the processes involved in the decision making.

Writing in the 1960s and 1970s, the structuralists are all experts on Soviet policy. They are mostly Sovietologists intent on examining the Russian motives that led to the decision to emplace Soviet missiles in Cuba in 1962.

While the official motives for the Soviets emplacing missiles in Cuba in 1962 may never be known, Nikita Khrushchev provides some tenuous reasons in his memoir. The initial volume was published in 1970 and is entitled *Khrushchev Remembers*.[1] The sequel was published in 1974 as *Khrushchev Remembers: The Last Testament*.[2] More official and authentic is the account of the crisis contained in Anatolii Gromyko's *Through Russian Eyes* (1973).[3]

According to Khrushchev in his initial account, the Soviet Union attempted to install missiles in Cuba primarily to "restrain the United States from precipitous military action against Castro's government."[4] Furthermore, the Soviet Union expected that the missiles "would have equalized . . . the balance of power."[5] The one point that Khrushchev emphasizes is that by the emplacement of ballistic missiles in Cuba, the

Russians did not seek to start a war. On the contrary, the principal aim of the Soviets was only to deter the United States from starting a war in Cuba.[6]

Khrushchev maintains that the Soviet Union only sought to protect Cuba as a socialist country, as an example to other Latin American countries. It was believed that if Cuba fell to U.S. imperialism, then other Latin American countries would reject Marxism.[7]

Why did the Soviet Union finally agree to remove the missiles from Cuba? Khrushchev claims that intelligence evidence indicated that Kennedy might have to take military action to stay in power. It was believed that if he did not take military action, then the military would overthrow him. The entire situation would then be out of control. Thus the Soviet Union decided to make concessions in the interest of peace.[8]

In *Khrushchev Remembers: The Last Testament*, the Premier further explains the rationale for the Soviet withdrawal of the missiles. In this sequel, Khrushchev claims that the Soviet Union promised to withdraw its missiles from Cuba in exchange for a U.S. promise to withdraw its missiles from Turkey and Italy. By agreeing to these symbolic measures, the President created the impression of mutual concessions.[9] Kennedy therefore became someone the Soviets could trust.[10]

Khrushchev contends that both he and President Kennedy behaved as statesmen; they did not become reckless but rather terminated the crisis by compromise.[11] According to the Premier, the compromise proved to be a great Soviet victory, for Cuba continued to exist "in front of the open jaws of predatory American imperialism."[12]

In his *Through Russian Eyes*, Gromyko (professor at the Soviet Academy of the Sciences) charges that the roots of the Cuban missile crisis "lay in the aspirations of the United States to secure for itself a monopolistic right to security, while denying the right of self-defense to other peoples."[13] The Cuban crisis began with the U-2 flights over Cuba, and it continued when the United States decided to exploit the situation of the missiles in Cuba even though the missiles did not alter the balance of nuclear power.[14]

According to Gromyko, the Soviet Union decided to install

missiles in Cuba only after the United States had repeatedly rejected Soviet proposals that U.S. bases and missiles be liquidated in foreign countries.[15] The U.S. response to the Soviet missiles "threatened tens of millions of people with atomic death."[16] Russia decided, therefore, that it had an obligation to the world to preserve the peace, a peace jeopardized by reckless U.S. imperialism. "Thus, Moscow offered Washington peace instead of thermonuclear war."[17]

According to the Russian perspective, as enunciated by Khrushchev and Gromyko, the primary motive for emplacing Soviet missiles in Cuba was purportedly to protect Cuba from a U.S. invasion. Secondary motives, however, are apparent. Besides protecting Cuba, the Soviets sought to equalize the nuclear balance of power and to secure the removal of U.S. missiles in foreign countries.

The official U.S. perspective of the Soviet motives at the time of the crisis was somewhat different, according to Theodore Sorensen. In his book, *Kennedy*, Sorensen states that the President considered five possible Soviet motives.[18] For the President, the emplacement of Soviet missiles in Cuba was intended probably to do one of the following: (1) to test U.S. resolve in the politics of the Cold War, (2) to divert U.S. attention away from Berlin, (3) to defend Cuba, (4) to provide leverage for bargaining a settlement on Berlin in exchange for a withdrawal of U.S. overseas bases, and (5) to alter the nuclear balance of power.[19] While the President gave some credence to the third and fifth possible motives, he gave primary credence to the first. Kennedy therefore believed that the primary Soviet motives for emplacing missiles in Cuba were to test U.S. resolve and to secure a Soviet political victory in the Cold War.[20]

One of the earliest accounts by Sovietologists in which the Russian motives were analyzed was *Strategic Power and Soviet Foreign Policy* (1965) by Arnold L. Horelick and Myron Rush, analysts for the RAND Corporation.[21] These two experts on Soviet foreign policy contend that the emplacement of missiles in Cuba was a bold attempt by the Russians to alter the strategic balance of nuclear power, and thereby to reinforce the worldwide position of the Soviet Union.[22] The successful emplacement of operational missiles in Cuba would have im-

proved the nuclear strike capabilities of the Soviets by improv-
ing their preemptive attack potential.[23]

Horelick and Rush dismiss the Khrushchev and Gromyko
contention that the primary reason for emplacing nuclear missiles in Cuba was to protect the small socialist country from a
U.S. attack. They also dismiss the argument of some that the
Soviet Union sought to use Cuba as a means of securing the
removal of missiles in Turkey. Finally, they counter the conviction of those who believe that Berlin was actually the major
target of the Soviets.[24] U.S. strategic superiority "made it too
risky for the Soviet Union to use or even threaten to use Berlin
as a trump card."[25] The Soviet effort to deploy strategic missiles in Cuba was essentially a typical Russian strategy of bluff
and deception to improve the Soviet strategic nuclear position.[26] It was this failure in bluff and deception directed against
the West that contributed to Khrushchev's removal from power.[27]

According to Horelick and Rush, the Soviets initially hoped
that the United States would be presented with a fait accompli
in Cuba, like the concrete wall in Berlin. Instead, the Soviet
Union was presented with a U.S. fait accompli, the quarantine.
By directing action against the Russians, the United States
compelled the Soviets to act quickly. Confronted with the speed
and resolution of the United States, the Soviets had to decide
whether to resort to violence. Fear that the United States was
planning an imminent act of force against Cuba compelled
Khrushchev to act.[28] "Manifest strategic superiority made it im-
possible for the Soviet forces to deter an American attack on
Cuba, so that withdrawal was the only path . . . " consistent
with a policy of avoiding a general war.[29]

Power in the Kremlin (1969) by Michael Tatu, a French Sovietologist, is a political study of Russian leadership that focuses
on a few powerful men in the Kremlin and their thirst for greater
power as evidenced by the U-2 crisis and, especially, the Cuban missile crisis.[30] The account is an intriguing study of conflict within the walls of the Kremlin.

Tatu, like Horelick and Rush, dismisses the defense of Cuba
as the primary motive behind the Soviet decision to introduce
ballistic missiles in Cuba in the fall of 1962. According to Tatu,
if the defense of Cuba were the primary reason for the missiles,

then the Soviets could have taken less drastic action. They could have extended the Warsaw Pact guarantees of collective action against foreign aggression to Cuba, or they could have made public declaration of intent to go to war on behalf of Cuba in case of aggression.[31]

Tatu contends that the decision to emplace Soviet missiles in Cuba was the gamble of one man, Khrushchev, and the aim of his scheme was a financially inexpensive means of altering the strategic balance of power. The real objective behind Khrushchev's gamble was a favorable Soviet settlement of the Berlin issue, for his prestige within the Kremlin depended upon Berlin. Thus, Khrushchev hoped to intimidate the United States by altering the strategic balance of nuclear power. Through such intimidation, Khrushchev sought to effect a settlement on Berlin; such a diplomatic victory would have consolidated Khrushchev's leadership position.[32]

While Berlin was clearly Khrushchev's objective, he knew that he could not take unilateral action against Berlin; such was illegal and would be condemned. Any unilateral action by the Soviets in Berlin would be cause for war. However, there was nothing illegal in emplacing missiles in Cuba. If such an operation were successful, then Khrushchev reasoned that he could bargain with the United States on Berlin and perhaps also on U.S. nuclear bases in Turkey.[33]

According to Tatu, the announcement by the United States to respond to the Soviet missiles in Cuba with a quarantine caused a power confrontation within the Kremlin that was reflected in the headlines of the daily news. The following headlines from *Pravda* indicate a vacillation between aggressive and conciliatory policies, a vacillation reflective of a power struggle:

The unleashed American aggressors must be stopped! (10/24)

Hands off Cuba! (10/24)

The aggresive designs of United States imperialists must be foiled. Peace on earth must be defended and strengthened! (10/25)

Everything to prevent war. (10/26)

Reason must prevail. (10/26)

Peoples of all countries, be vigilant; unmask the imperialist warmon-

gers! Struggle most actively for the preservation of a durable and in-
destructible peace! (10/27)

We must defend and consolidate peace on earth. (10/28)

We must ensure the peace and security of all peoples. (10/29)[34]

Tatu suggests that Khrushchev, who favored conciliation by
October 26th, was outvoted, and his colleagues took a stronger
position by October 27th. Khrushchev may not have consulted
his colleagues when he wrote his "personal" letter. Thus, the
second "formal" letter issued by the collective leadership requested the removal of missiles from Turkey. The stiffening of
the Kremlin position reflected the disarray between Khrushchev and his associates behind the Kremlin walls.[35]

Why did the Soviet Union ultimately retreat? The Soviets realized that Kennedy was not bluffing as Khrushchev had done.
They also became aware that U.S. military pressure was con-
verging on the Soviet Union. Yet, most importantly, Soviet intelligence became convinced that the United States might attack Cuba, destroy all the missiles, and overthrow the Castro
regime. Destruction of socialist Cuba would be a catastrophic
defeat for communism and for the prestige of the Soviet Union.[36]

Tatu believes that the Cuban crisis marked the termination
of the great Soviet design on Berlin. It ended the rocket-rattling
tactics that had served Khrushchev so well since the launching
of Sputnik in 1957.[37] Finally, the Cuban crisis caused Khrushchev to lose ground suddenly within the collective leadership.
The personal attacks leveled at him during the crisis would lead
ultimately to his downfall.[38]

In *The Rivals*, (1971), Adam B. Ulam presents an ingenious
new theory that attempts to explain the Russian motives for
allowing the missiles to be emplaced in Cuba in the fall of 1962.[39]
Ulam, research professor at the Russian Center of Harvard,
contends that the major threat to the security of the Soviet Union
in 1962 was not the foreign policy of the United States but the
policies of the Chinese. "The Soviets wanted to force not only
the United States to agree on a German peace treaty with absolute prohibition of nuclear weapons for Bonn, but also
China."[40] Thus, by one bold operation, the Soviets sought to
achieve two separate objectives.

According to Ulam, Khrushchev may have intended to demand that the United States repudiate its protection of For-
mosa in exchange for removal of the missiles in Cuba. Khrushchev also may have believed that the Chinese would have been
forced to sign a nuclear nonproliferation treaty when confronted by the dazzling Cuba operation, by a U.N. resolution
endorsing a U.S.-Soviet agreement on nonproliferation, and by
a threat of joint U.S. and Soviet action against any violator of
the nonproliferation treaty.[41]

How was this to be accomplished? Ulam claims that the Soviets had hoped that the missiles would not be discovered. Then,
in late November, Khrushchev would have gone to the United
Nations to announce to a startled world the news of Soviet
operational missiles to Cuba:

> The shock of the news would be almost immediately followed by re-
> lief, for the Soviet Union would propose a far-reaching settlement of
> the outstanding world problems, a vast diminution of the danger of a
> nuclear conflict which had hung over the world since 1949. The U.S.S.R.
> would pull out the deadly weapons in exchange for the United States
> agreeing on a peace treaty with Germany and on atom-free zones in
> Central Europe and the Pacific; other countries would pledge nuclear
> abstinence. The Americans' bitterness at having been deceived would
> be assuaged by the knowledge that the Chinese acquisition of nuclear
> weapons could be postponed indefinitely. The Chinese rancor could
> be overcome by demonstrating that it was not through secret collusion
> with the United States but by a bold aggressive policy that Russia was
> exacting this settlement.[42]

Based on the above scenario, Ulam discounts the possibility
that the crisis was an attempt by the Soviet Union to redress
the balance of nuclear power, to protect Cuba, or to strengthen
the Soviet position on Berlin. "The magnitude of the risk involved clearly indicates that much, much more must have been
at stake."[43]

Contrary to Tatu, Ulam does not believe that the second Russian "formal" letter of October 27th to President Kennedy represented the dictates of a collective leadership that had
triumphed over Khrushchev. Neither did the formal letter represent a stiffening of the Soviet position. Rather, the second

letter, containing the suggestion of an exchange of Soviet missiles in Cuba for U.S. missiles in Turkey, indicated that the Chairman was ready to capitulate.[44]

The successful termination of the missile crisis, according to Ulam, did not mark the end of the Cold War. It did terminate, however, that acute phase of the Cold War that had begun in 1958 when the Soviets commenced putting pressure on Berlin for a German treaty.[45]

In a 1972 *Political Science Quarterly* article, "The Cuban Missile Crisis: A Study of Its Strategic Context," Sovietologists Jerome H. Kahan and Anne K. Long state that Nikita Khrushchev's primary motive in introducing nuclear missiles into Cuba was the Premier's "desire to rapidly rectify the strategic balance."[46] Since the late 1950s, the Soviet Union had been encircled by U.S. missiles in Turkey, Italy, and England. By emplacing intermediate-range ballistic missiles in Cuba, the Soviet Union intended to present to the United States a dramatic counter to this threat that would underscore the Russian concern over U.S. bases abroad.[47]

According to Kahan and Long, the Soviet missiles in Cuba did complicate a U.S. nuclear attack although they were vulnerable to such an attack. Because of their close range, the missiles could bypass the U.S. nuclear warning system, and, thus, they presented a danger to U.S. SAC bombers. The missiles also posed a new threat to cities in Latin America that until October 1962 had been considered beyond the range of Soviet intercontinental ballistic missiles. Hence, the Soviet missiles in Cuba did strengthen the Soviet nuclear deterrent force.[48]

While maintaining the strategic significance of Khrushchev's decision, Kahan and Long concede that other motivational factors may have been a desire: (1) to secure a settlement of the Berlin issue, (2) to demonstrate to the world the strength of Soviet military and foreign policy, and (3) to protect Cuba from an invasion. The coauthors also concede that Khrushchev may have been hoping to repair his own prestige by degrading U.S. strategic power.[49]

Kahan and Long claim that U.S. preponderance of strategic nuclear power both initiated and concluded the crisis. The Kennedy administration's emphasis on nuclear superiority tilted the balance of power so far against the Soviets that they were compelled to emplace missiles in Cuba so as to rectify the strategic imbalance. The combined strategic and conventional superiority of the United States, however, contributed greatly to Khrushchev's decision to withdraw the Soviet missiles in Cuba. The preponderance of U.S. strategic power negated the Soviet strategic capabilities, making the use of nuclear weapons by the Soviet leaders irrational.[50]

In *The Making of a Missile Crisis* (1976), Herbert S. Dinerstein, professor of Sovietology at Johns Hopkins University, contends that both Kennedy and Khrushchev frightened the world needlessly with the threat of nuclear war.[51] Both used brinkmanship diplomacy for their own ends. Nuclear war was possible only if the Soviet Union took direct action against the United States because of Cuba or if the United States took direct action against the Soviet Union because of Berlin. Thus the crisis taught the world that nuclear war could be avoided despite a long history of mutual misunderstanding.[52]

The Soviet Union emplaced missiles in Cuba in order to alter the balance of nuclear power, to protect Cuba, to deter a U.S. attack, to improve the position of the Soviet Union on Berlin, and to assert Soviet leadership over other socialist countries.[53] In deploying missiles in Cuba, Khrushchev failed to anticipate the proper U.S. response. Khrushchev apparently believed that what he wanted to happen would happen. "A rational Khrushchev should have anticipated what [actually] happened."[54]

Dinerstein suggests that the United States could tolerate a gradual change in the balance of nuclear power, but it could not permit a sudden change that would have produced sharp political changes.[55] "If the measure of the balance of power was the capacity to create millions of corpses in a half hour, missiles in Cuba would have given the Soviet Union something like instant equality."[56]

How were the missiles to be used to get what the Soviet Union wanted? The Russian leadership had hoped that the missiles would be operational before their discovery. Then the United States would be faced with a fait accompli. A retreat of the United States from Soviet brinkmanship would have effected a change in the balance of power, provided protection to Cuba, prevented a U.S. attack on Cuba, and increased the prestige of the Soviet Union in world communism. Even if brinkmanship failed, the Soviets could employ bargaining strategy. In exchange for the removal of missiles, the Soviet Union could demand U.S. recognition of the socialist regime of Cuba's Castro. Such action still would have increased Soviet prestige in the contest for world leadership of communism.[57]

The Soviet Union failed to consider the possibility that President Kennedy would not back down to intimidation. Kennedy firmly believed that the missiles threatened U.S. security, and, thus, he responded strongly to the threat. While Kennedy worried about nuclear war, he used the threat of such as leverage against the Soviet Union as well as against opponents of his course of action within his administration.[58]

The Sovietologist interpreters of the Cuban missile crisis generally lack unanimity in their perspective. Yet it is interesting to note that not a single one gives direct credence to the contention of the Kennedy administration that the primary Soviet motivation for the missile venture was to test U.S. will and resolve and to secure a political triumph in the politics of the Cold War. Furthermore, only two of the Soviet experts give any credence to the Khrushchev and Gromyko contentions that the Soviet Union deployed missiles to Cuba to defend the tiny socialist country from a U.S. attack (Kahan, Dinerstein); two other interpreters emphatically deny such Soviet motivation (Horelick, Ulam).

The general consensus of these interpreters is that the primary motive behind the Soviet missile maneuver in Cuba was to alter or equalize the strategic balance of nuclear power (Horelick, Tatu, Kahan, Dinerstein). Other hypotheses are: (1) the Soviets sought to reassert their prestige and authority as the leader in international communism (Horelick, Kahan, Dinerstein); (2) the Russians sought to strengthen their bargaining position on Berlin (Tatu, Kahan, Dinerstein); and (3) the Soviets sought to prevent China from securing nuclear weapons by a nonproliferation treaty with the United States establishing atom-free zones in Central Europe and in the Pacific (Ulam).

Why did the Soviets ultimately agree to withdraw the missiles? Considering the overall nuclear superiority of the United States in the world and the overwhelming conventional military superiority of the United States in this hemisphere, the Russians had no other rational option than to remove the missiles. Perhaps the Soviets were induced to act because of the U.S. threat to attack Cuba by air and sea (Tatu).

The successful termination of the crisis ended the Soviet design to secure all of Berlin, and it undercut Khrushchev's power and prestige in the Soviet Union, which eventually led to his ouster as Chairman and Premier (Tatu, Ulam). The resolution of the crisis also resolved the doubts that people had regarding the ability of statesmen to avoid nuclear war despite a history of misunderstanding (Dinerstein).

NOTES

1. Nikita S. Khrushchev, *Khrushchev Remembers*, trans. Strobe Talbott (Boston: Little, Brown, 1970). The authenticity of this account has never been ascertained. The memoir contains numerous deceptions and evasions, and it omits many significant facts and circumstances. The memoir, however, is an interesting account of a man who appeared to have a split personality, a man of peace and a man of rage. For U.S. analyses of Khrushchev, see Carl A. Linden, *Khrushchev and the Soviet Leadership, 1957–1964* (Baltimore: Johns Hopkins University Press, 1966), and William Hyland and Richard W. Shyrock, *The Fall of Khrushchev* (New York: Funk and Wagnalls, 1968).

2. Nikita S. Khrushchev, *Khrushchev Remembers: The Last Testament*, trans. Strobe Talbott (Boston: Little, Brown, 1974). The authenticity of this account also has never been ascertained.

3. Anatolii A. Gromyko, *Through Russian Eyes: President Kennedy's 1036 Days* (Washington, D.C.: International Library, Inc., 1973).

4. Khrushchev, *Khrushchev Remembers*, p. 494.

5. *Ibid.*

6. *Ibid.*, p. 495.

7. *Ibid.*, p. 493.

8. *Ibid.*, pp. 497–99.

9. Khrushchev, *The Last Testament*, p. 512.

10. *Ibid.*, p. 513.

11. Khrushchev, *Khrushchev Remembers*, p. 504.

12. *Ibid.*, p. 505.

13. Gromyko, *Through Russian Eyes*, p. 171.

14. *Ibid.*, pp. 171–72.
15. *Ibid.*, pp. 172–76.
16. *Ibid.*, p. 177.
17. *Ibid.*, p. 180.
18. Theodore C. Sorensen, *Kennedy* (New York: Harper and Row, 1965; paperback ed., New York: Bantam Books, 1966).
19. *Ibid.*, pp. 762–64.
20. *Ibid.*, p. 764.
21. Arnold L. Horelick and Myron Rush, *Strategic Power and Soviet Foreign Policy* (Chicago: University of Chicago Press, 1965). See also, Arnold L. Horelick, "The Cuban Missile Crisis: An Analysis of Soviet Calculations and Behavior," *World Politics* 16 (April 1964): 364–77.
22. Horelick and Rush, *Strategic Power*, pp. 127, 136.
23. *Ibid.*, pp. 136–37.
24. *Ibid.*, pp. 127–39.
25. *Ibid.*, p. 140.
26. *Ibid.*, p. 141.
27. *Ibid.*, p. 156.
28. *Ibid.*, pp. 151–52.
29. *Ibid.*, p. 153.
30. Michael Tatu, *Power in the Kremlin: From Khrushchev to Kosygin*, trans. Helen Katel (New York: The Viking Press, 1969).
31. *Ibid.*, p. 230.
32. *Ibid.*, pp. 230–32.
33. *Ibid.*, p. 233.
34. *Ibid.*, p. 261.
35. *Ibid.*, pp. 268–70.
36. *Ibid.*, pp. 264–65.
37. *Ibid.*, pp. 270–74.
38. *Ibid.*, p. 275.
39. Adam B. Ulam, *The Rivals: America and Russia Since World War II* (New York: The Viking Press, 1971). This version follows the general theory originally presented by Ulam in *Expansion and Coexistence: The History of Soviet Foreign Policy, 1917–1967* (New York: Praeger Publishers, 1968).
40. Ulam, *The Rivals*, p. 329.
41. *Ibid.*
42. *Ibid.*, p. 331.
43. *Ibid.*, p. 332.
44. *Ibid.*, p. 335.
45. *Ibid.*, p. 336.
46. Jerome H. Kahan and Anne K. Long, "The Cuban Missile Cri-

sis: A Study of Its Strategic Context," *Political Science Quarterly* 87 (December 1972): 568.

47. *Ibid.*
48. *Ibid.*, pp. 568–71.
49. *Ibid.*, p. 569.
50. *Ibid.*, pp. 580–89.
51. Herbert S. Dinerstein, *The Making of a Missile Crisis: October 1962* (Baltimore: Johns Hopkins University Press, 1976).
52. *Ibid.*, pp. 229–33.
53. *Ibid.*, pp. 186–87.
54. *Ibid.*, p. 152.
55. *Ibid.*, pp. 155–58.
56. *Ibid.*, p. 157.
57. *Ibid.*, pp. 187–89.
58. *Ibid.*

8

CONCLUSION: ANOTHER INTERPRETATION, ANOTHER PERSPECTIVE

As the sun dawned over the sparkling blue waters of the serene Caribbean Sea on Sunday morning, October 14, 1962, Air Force Major Rudolf Anderson, Jr. made a routine reconnaissance flight over western Cuba. The film aboard the U-2 plane was processed and analyzed that evening in customary fashion. By Monday afternoon, however, the photographic interpreters discovered on the island the rude beginnings of Soviet-structured bases for medium-range ballistic missiles. Thus, inauspiciously began the Cuban missile crisis, a confrontation that seemed to carry the antagonists to the brink of nuclear holocaust, at least in appearance if not also in fact.

While the Soviet motives for the emplacement of nuclear missiles in Cuba in the autumn of 1962 may never be revealed, several reasons suggest themselves as possible motives for this adventurous maneuver. The primary impetus behind the Soviet gamble was to alter, however minutely, the strategic balance of nuclear power that overwhelmingly favored the United States. Any minor change in the nuclear status quo also would effect a change in the political balance of power, at least in appearance if not also in actuality.

Granted that the primary motive of the Soviets was to alter in some measure the balance of power in the world, what secondary motives prevailed in the Soviet decision? Some reasonable hypotheses are that the Soviets sought: (1) to defend Cuba

from another U.S. invasion, such as the Bay of Pigs; (2) to res-
urrect the prestige of the Soviet Union as the leader in international communism; (3) to strengthen the bargaining position
of the Soviet Union on a favorable settlement of the Berlin issue; and (4) to divert attention away from a host of Russian
domestic problems.

While Nikita Khrushchev and his Soviet comrades were justified in emplacing missiles in Cuba under international law,
they seriously miscalculated the U.S. response to such action.
Khrushchev believed that what he wanted to happen would
happen. He firmly believed that the United States would accept operational nuclear missiles in Cuba as a fait accompli.
Soviet intelligence assumed that the United States would either
protest and acquiesce or threaten and negotiate. The Russians
also miscalculated the solidarity of the Western hemispheric
nations to such a Soviet maneuver.

U.S. intelligence likewise made serious miscalculations. Intelligence experts in the United States assumed that Soviet policy was too cautious to place missiles in Castro's Cuba, especially since the Russians had never before permitted nuclear
missiles outside the borders of the Soviet Union. U.S. intelligence also assumed that Khrushchev, as a rational being, would
not undertake to emplace missiles in Cuba because such action
would be interpreted in the United States as irrational. Thus
intelligence experts seriously erred in believing that their assumptions conformed to reality.

Once the discovery of the missiles in Cuba was made known
to President Kennedy, he immediately assumed leadership of
the situation. He assembled around himself a group of key advisers, known as Ex Com, who discussed possible Soviet motives for the Cuban venture and formulated the U.S. response
to the Soviet emplacement of missiles in Cuba. While several
members of this ad hoc committee believed that the primary
motive was a Soviet desire to alter the strategic balance of power,
the President viewed the situation as a Soviet attempt to challenge his will and determination. Thus Kennedy believed he
had to react strongly.

There is no evidence to substantiate the Kennedy contention
that Khrushchev sought to challenge him personally. There also

is no evidence to substantiate Ex Com's contention that the missiles altered the strategic balance of power. First, while there is incontrovertible evidence that Soviet nuclear missiles were introduced into Cuba, there is no public evidence to date to indicate that there were nuclear warheads available for the missiles in Cuba. Second, while the missiles in Cuba did bypass the U.S. early warning ballistic missile system, this did not add substantially to the Soviet nuclear arsenal. In case of a Soviet attack on the United States, the missiles in Cuba would reach the United States first, which would provide ample time to deter missiles launched from the Soviet Union. If the missiles in the Soviet Union were launched first, then the United States would have sufficient time to liquidate the missiles in Cuba. The Soviet missiles in Cuba, therefore, did not truly alter the strategic balance of power; they only complicated the U.S. response to a possible nuclear attack.

What the Soviet missiles would have represented had they remained in Cuba was a psychological victory for the Soviet Union. They would have changed the political balance of power in appearance, and this change would have occurred in an area of vital interest to the United States.

While President Kennedy declared the missiles in Cuba to be offensive, this was an arbitrary and superficial declaration. There was no difference between the Soviet offensive missiles in Cuba and the so-called U.S. defensive missiles in Turkey, Italy, and England. Yet, by defining the missiles in Cuba as offensive, President Kennedy was able to accuse the Russians of deception, for Khrushchev had stated that he would not introduce offensive missiles into Cuba. Furthermore, by defining the missiles as offensive, Kennedy was able to treat an international political matter as a military incident and, therefore, as a threat to U.S. security.

During the covert national phase of the crisis, the President and the members of Ex Com discussed four possible alternative responses to the Soviet emplacement of missiles in the Western Hemisphere. These options ranged from doing nothing to an air strike and an invasion of Cuba. The advocates of a firm military response in the form of an air strike or an invasion initially dominated the ad hoc committee's proceedings. To the credit of the President, he opted for a more moderate response. In collaboration with his advisers, Kennedy elected to implement a naval blockade, which he euphemistically called a quarantine. Is this not, however, a military response? Under international law a unilateral blockade is considered a military action. While the United Nations Charter provides for collective hemispheric action, such approval was obtained from the Organization of American States after the fact, after the President had announced on October 22 his intention to impose a blockade. While the participants in the Ex Com deliberations defended the implementation of a blockade as a flexible and reasonable measure, a half-way measure between doing nothing and an air strike, it was, nonetheless, a military response to a political situation.

If the Soviet missiles in Cuba represented a political rather than a strategic alteration in the balance of power, as the President believed, then why did he opt for a military response? Why did he reject a politically diplomatic approach, such as negotiating the removal of U.S.missiles in Turkey in exchange for the Soviet missiles in Cuba as suggested on October 20 by Adlai Stevenson, U.S. Ambassador to the United Nations?

The Kennedy administration maintained that it rejected private diplomatic negotiations because the Soviet action of emplacing missiles in Cuba was a drastic policy requiring a firm reaction, a determined and visible U.S. response. Such a response was essential to preserve American values and world peace as well as the credibility of U.S. defense commitments throughout the free world. Administration officials also claimed that a U.S. diplomatic and negotiated policy would have put the Soviets in control of events rather than the United States. According to the participants, a successful resolution of the crisis required the United States to control the confrontation. Kennedy, therefore, rejected all diplomatic approaches to resolving the missile crisis.

While President Kennedy believed that he had to react immediately and forcibly to the Russian missile scheme, the reasons for such belief were other than those officially stated. First, the President believed that the missiles in Cuba represented an attempt by the Soviets to test not only the will and determination of the United States but his own personal will and determination. Such a personal challenge required a vigorous response. Second, Kennedy needed to remove the missiles from Cuba in order to achieve a victory in foreign policy before the November elections if the Democrats were to be successful in the 1962 political campaign. Such a requirement necessitated an immediate response. These considerations, one personal and the other political, dictated an immediate and forceful response; they also were the bases upon which the President rejected a prolonged, diplomatic, and negotiated approach to the Soviet emplacement of missiles in Cuba.

No crisis or confrontation existed publicly until Monday, October 22. That evening, President Kennedy went before the television cameras to announce the discovery of the Soviet missiles in Cuba. By defining the missiles as offensive, and hence a threat to U.S. security, the President raised the Cuban episode to the level of a crisis. By announcing the implementation of a blockade, a military response, Kennedy raised the missile situation to the level of a confrontation. Thus, while Khrushchev was responsible for irresponsibly emplacing missiles in Cuba, despite his internationally legal right to do so, Kennedy was responsible for irresponsibly creating a crisis atmosphere and for raising the crisis to the level of confrontation.

After having initiated the confrontation, President Kennedy acted responsibly during most of the week of the international crisis. As President and as Commander-in-Chief, Kennedy exercised responsible leadership. He acted cautiously; he was neither reckless nor hasty in his decisions. He tried to control the situation in spite of bureaucratic politics. Yet, by the end of the week, he still refused to negotiate a settlement and was prepared to go to the brink; he gave serious consideration to bombing the Soviet missile bases in Cuba if the crisis was not resolved by Tuesday, October 30.

If Kennedy had decided to bomb the missile sites in Cuba and if the crisis had not been resolved successfully before October 30, the world status quo would have been altered irreparably. If the United States had bombed the Soviet missile sites in Cuba, some Russians undoubtedly would have been killed. Khrushchev then would have been compelled to retaliate. The Soviets probably would have bombed the U.S. missile bases in Turkey, killing some Americans. The United States then would have been forced to retaliate via bombing some missile bases inside the Soviet Union. An unavoidable Russian response would have thrust the world toward thermonuclear holocaust.

While the above scenario was unlikely to happen, it was a possibility. There was perhaps a one in three chance of it transpiring. Such is most sobering. Fortunately for the world, Khrushchev decided to withdraw the Soviet missiles from Cuba before such a scenario transpired. The confrontation was resolved successfully on Sunday morning, October 28, when Khrushchev announced his decision to withdraw the missiles from the Caribbean island in exchange for a U.S. pledge not to invade Cuba.

Why did Khrushchev decide to withdraw the Soviet missiles from Cuba? Considering the overall nuclear superiority of the United States in the world and the overwhelming conventional military superiority of the United States in the Western Hemisphere, the Chairman had no other rational option than to withdraw the missiles. The specific incident that induced Khrushchev to act was Robert Kennedy's statement to Soviet Ambassador Dobrynin of Saturday night, October 27, that it was essential that the missiles be withdrawn immediately. The Attorney General instructed the Soviet Ambassador that the United States would remove the Russian missiles in Cuba unless the Soviets withdrew their missiles instantaneously. It was this explicit threat of further U.S. military action, combined with the Attorney General's promise that the President would withdraw the U.S. missiles in Turkey after the resolution of the crisis, that impelled Khrushchev to announce the next day the Soviet decision to withdraw the Russian missiles.

Two incidents occurred on Saturday, October 27, which could have triggered possible nuclear responses. It is to the credit of both Kennedy and Khrushchev that both exercised caution and that neither one retaliated. The first incident was the shooting down by the Soviets of Major Anderson's U-2 reconnaissance plane over Cuba on Saturday morning. Against the advice of the Joint Chiefs of Staff, the President refused to attack Cuba immediately.

Almost simultaneously, half way around the world, another U.S. reconnaissance pilot had strayed accidentally into Soviet air space. While the pilot barely avoided a confrontation with Soviet fighter planes, Khrushchev wondered whether the incident was a prelude to a U.S. attack. Yet, rather than immediately responding via some form of retaliation, Khrushchev acted responsibly and exercised extreme caution.

The two incidents well illustrate how perilously close to the nuclear abyss the world stood. Despite the efforts of Kennedy and Khrushchev to control the crisis situation, the two incidents demonstrate how little control each one had over the events. Although the probability of nuclear war via rational choice may have been low, that of nuclear war via a Strangelovian incident was high. It is possible that the Cuban missile crisis could have led to nuclear war, not because of rational choice but because of human error. Such is the irrationality inherent in international nuclear confrontations.

The successful termination of the Cuban missile crisis had mixed consequences. As a result of the confrontation, the Soviets ended their design to secure all of Berlin and embarked upon a policy of peaceful coexistence. The crisis also undercut Khrushchev's power and prestige within the Politburo, which ultimately led to his ouster as Chairman and Premier.

While a superficial détente ensued after the crisis, symbolized by the installation of the teletype hot line between the White House and the Kremlin and by the signing of a nuclear test ban treaty that limited atmospheric tests, both the United States and the Soviet Union embarked upon a new nuclear arms race, an arms race that is continuing today. Also, contrary to the administration's belief that bold U.S. action in the crisis would strengthen credibility among its allies and NATO, the opposite transpired. Because of the unilateral action of the United States during the crisis, Charles de Gaulle eventually withdrew France from NATO, thus effectively weakening the multinational organization.

As a consequence of the crisis, the United States gained a

renewed confidence in its military power, but such confidence soon became arrogance; this arrogance of power eventually led the United States to escalate its action in Vietnam. Finally, the so-called Kennedy triumph in the nuclear confrontation led the American people to seek military solutions to purely international political problems.

While many interpreters of the Cuban missile crisis ascribe the lack of armed conflict in the confrontation to the skillful and cautious management of the situation by both President Kennedy and Chairman Khrushchev, credit also must be given to plain dumb luck. The vagaries of the nuclear age, especially in a military confrontation, did not permit crisis control with any high degree of certitude. The risks of accident, miscalculation, human error, or irrationality are calculable only to a limited degree. In the final analysis the world's first nuclear confrontation was terminated successfully without armed conflict or catastrophic consequences as much by fortune as by human design.

BIBLIOGRAPHY

GOVERNMENT DOCUMENTS

U.S. Congress. House. Committee on Appropriations. *Hearings on Department of Defense Appropriations for 1964.* 88th Cong., 1st sess., 1963.
————. House. Committee on Armed Services. *Hearings on Military Posture.* 88th Cong., 1st sess., 1963.
————. Senate. Preparedness Investigation Subcommittee of the Committee on Armed Services. *Interim Report on Cuban Military Buildup.* 88th Cong., 1st sess., 1963.
U.S. Department of State. *American Foreign Policy: Current Documents, 1962.* Washington, D.C.: Historical Office of Bureau of Public Affairs, U.S. Government Printing Office, 1966.
————. "Messages Exchanged by President Kennedy and Chairman Khrushchev During the Cuban Missile Crisis of October 1962." *Bulletin 69* (November 19, 1973): 635–54. Washington, D.C.: U.S. Government Printing Office, 1973.
————. "The Soviet Threat to the Americans." *Bulletin 47* (November 12, 1962): 715–47. Washington, D.C.: U.S. Government Printing Office, 1962.
————. "President Kennedy on Cuba." *Bulletin 47* (December 10, 1962): 874–75. Washington, D.C.: U.S. Government Printing Office, 1962.
————. *Events in United States-Cuban Relations: A Chronology, 1957–1963.* Washington, D.C.: U.S. Government Printing Office, 1963.

U.S. President. *Public Papers of the Presidents of the United States*: John
     F. Kennedy, 1962. Washington, D.C.: Office of the Federal Reg-
     ister, U.S. Government Printing Office.

MANUSCRIPT SOURCES

Kennedy, John F. *Personal and Public Papers*. Boston: John F. Kennedy
     Library.

NEWSPAPERS

Current Digest of the Soviet Press 14 (October 8, 1962-January 16, 1963).
Izvestia (Moscow), September 12,-December 24, 1962.
New York Times, October 22,-November 20, 1962.
Pravda (Moscow), September 12,-December 24, 1962.
Washington Post, October 22,-November 20, 1962.

BOOKS

Abel, Elie. *The Missile Crisis*. Philadelphia: J. B. Lippincott, 1966.
————. *The Missiles of October: The Story of the Cuban Missile Crisis, 1962*.
     London: MacGibbon and Kee, 1969.
Allison, Graham T. *Essence of Decision: Explaining the Cuban Missile Cri-
     sis*. Boston: Little, Brown, 1971.
Art, Robert J., and Waltz, Kenneth N., eds. *The Use of Force: Interna-
     tional Politics and Foreign Policy*. Boston: Little, Brown, 1971.
Beggs, Robert, ed. *The Cuban Missile Crisis*. London: Longman Group
     Limited, 1971.
Bernstein, Barton J. "The Cuban Missile Crisis." In *Reflections on the
     Cold War: A Quarter Century of American Foreign Policy*, pp. 108–
     42. Edited by Lynn H. Miller and Ronald W. Pruessen. Phila-
     delphia: Temple University Press, 1974.
Bethel, Paul D. *The Losers: The Definitive Report, by an Eyewitness, of the
     Communist Conquest of Cuba and the Soviet Penetration in Latin
     America*. New Rochelle, N.Y.: Arlington House, 1969.
Bonsal, Philip W. *Cuba, Castro, and the United States*. Pittsburgh: Uni-
     versity of Pittsburgh Press, 1971.
Borisov, Oleg B., and Koloskov, B. T. *Soviet-Chinese Relations, 1945–
     1970*. Bloomington: Indiana University Press, 1975.
Brown, Seyom. *The Faces of Power: Constancy and Change in United States*

Foreign Policy from Truman to Johnson. New York: Columbia University Press, 1968.

Brune, Lester H. *The Missile Crisis of October 1962: A Review of Issues and References*. Claremont, Calif.: Regina Books, 1985.

Chayes, Abram. *The Cuban Missile Crisis: International Crisis and the Role of Law*. New York: Oxford University Press, 1974.

Clinch, Nancy Gager. *The Kennedy Neurosis*. New York: Grosset and Dunlap, 1973.

Cook, Fred J. *Cuban Missile Crisis, October 1962: The U.S. and Russia Face a Nuclear Showdown*. New York: F. Watts, 1972.

Crisp, Norman J. *The Brink*. New York: Pocket Books, 1983.

Daniel, James, and Hubbell, John G. *Strike in the West: The Complete Story of the Cuban Crisis*. New York: Holt, Rinehart and Winston, 1963.

Detzer, David. *The Brink: Cuban Missile Crisis, 1962*. New York: Crowell, 1979.

Dinerstein, Herbert S. *The Making of a Missile Crisis: October 1962*. Baltimore: Johns Hopkins University Press, 1976.

Divine, Robert A., ed. *The Cuban Missile Crisis*. Chicago: Quadrangle Books, 1971.

Dominguez, Jorge I. *Cuba: Order and Revolution*. Cambridge, Mass.: Harvard University Press, 1978.

Donald, Aida DiPace, ed. *John F. Kennedy and the New Frontier*. New York: Hill and Wang, 1966.

Dulles, Eleanor L., and Crane, Robert D., eds. *Detente: Cold War Strategies in Transition*. New York: Frederick A. Praeger, 1965.

Edmonds, Robin. *Soviet Foreign Policy, 1962–73: The Paradox of Super Power*. New York: Oxford University Press, 1975.

Fairlie, Henry. *The Kennedy Promise: The Politics of Expectation*. Garden City, N.Y.: Doubleday, 1973.

FitzSimons, Louise. *The Kennedy Doctrine*. New York: Random House, 1972.

Foreign Policy Association. *The Cuban Crisis: A Documentary Record*. New York: Foreign Policy Association, 1963.

George, Alexander L. "The Cuban Missile Crisis, 1962." In *The Limits of Coercive Diplomacy: Laos, Cuba, Vietnam*, pp. 86–143. Edited by Alexander L. George, David K. Hall, and William E. Simons. Boston: Little, Brown, 1971.

———, and Smoke, Richard. *Deterrence in American Foreign Policy: Theory and Practice*. New York: Columbia University Press, 1974.

Goodwin, Roberts A., ed. *Beyond the Cold War*. Chicago: Rand McNally, 1965.

Greene, Fred. "The Intelligence Arm: The Cuban Missile Crisis." In *Foreign Policy in the Sixties: The Issues and the Instruments*, pp. 127–40. Edited by Roger Hilsman and Robert C. Good. Baltimore: Johns Hopkins University Press, 1965.

Griffiths, John. *The Cuban Missile Crisis*. Vero Beach, Fla.: Rourke Enterprises, 1987.

Gromyko, Anatolii A. *Through Russian Eyes: President Kennedy's 1036 Days*. Washington, D.C.: International Library, 1973.

Halle, Louis J. *The Cold War as History*. New York: Harper and Row, 1967.

Halper, Thomas. *Foreign Policy Crises: Appearance and Reality in Decision Making*. Columbus, Ohio: Charles E. Merrill Publishing Company, 1971.

Halperin, Maurice. *The Rise and Decline of Fidel Castro: An Essay in Contemporary History*. Berkeley: University of California Press, 1972.

Harriman, W. Averell. *America and Russia in a Changing World*. New York: Doubleday, 1971.

Heath, Jim F. *Decade of Disillusionment: The Kennedy-Johnson Years*. Bloomington: Indiana University Press, 1975.

Hilsman, Roger. *To Move a Nation: The Politics of Foreign Policy in the Administration of John F. Kennedy*. Garden City, N.Y.: Doubleday, 1967.

Horelick, Arnold L., and Rush, Myron. *Strategic Power and Soviet Foreign Policy*. Chicago: University of Chicago Press, 1965.

Horowitz, David. *The Free World Colossus: A Critique of American Foreign Policy in the Cold War*. New York: Hill and Wang, 1965.

Hyland, William, and Shyrock, Richard W. *The Fall of Khrushchev*. New York: Funk and Wagnalls, 1968.

Ions, Edmund S., ed. *The Politics of John F. Kennedy*. New York: Barnes and Noble, 1967.

Jackson, D. Bruce. *Castro, the Kremlin, and Communism in Latin America*. Baltimore: Johns Hopkins University Press, 1969.

Kennedy, Robert F. *Thirteen Days: A Memoir of the Cuban Missile Crisis*. New York: W. W. Norton, 1969.

Khrushchev, Nikita S. *Khrushchev Remembers*. Translated by Strobe Talbott. Boston: Little, Brown, 1970.

———. *Khrushchev Remembers: The Last Testament*. Translated by Strobe Talbott. Boston: Little, Brown, 1974.

Kolkowicz, Roman. *The Soviet Military and the Communist Party*. Princeton, N.J.: Princeton University Press, 1967.

Krock, Arthur. *Memoirs: Sixty Years on the Firing Line*. New York: Funk and Wagnalls, 1968.

Lane, Thomas A. *The Leadership of President Kennedy*. Caldwell, Idaho: The Caxton Printers, 1964.

Langley, Lester D. *The Cuban Policy of the United States: A Brief History*. New York: John Wiley, 1968.

————. *The United States, Cuba, and Cold War: American Failure or Communist Conspiracy?* Lexington, Mass.: D. C. Heath, 1970.

Larson, David L., ed. *The Cuban Crisis of 1962: Selected Documents, Chronology, and Bibliography*. 2nd ed. Lanham, Md.: University Press of America, 1986.

Latham, Earl, ed. *J. F. Kennedy and Presidential Power*. Lexington, Mass.: D. C. Heath, 1972.

Lazo, Mario. *Dagger in the Heart: American Policy Failures in Cuba*. New York: Funk and Wagnalls, 1968.

LeFeber, Walter. *America, Russia, and the Cold War, 1945–1975*. 3rd ed. New York: John Wiley, 1976.

Lens, Sidney. *The Military-Industrial Complex*. Kansas City: Pilgrim Press, 1970.

Lieberson, Goddard, ed. *John Fitzgerald Kennedy, As We Remember Him*. New York: Atheneum, 1965.

Linden, Carl A. *Khrushchev and the Soviet Leadership, 1957–1964*. Baltimore: Johns Hopkins University Press, 1966.

Mankiewicz, Frank, and Jones, Kirby. *With Fidel: A Portrait of Castro and Cuba*. Chicago: Playboy Press, 1975.

McSherry, James E. *Khrushchev and Kennedy in Retrospect*. Palo Alto, Calif.: Open-Door Press, 1971.

Medvedev, Roy, and Medvedev, Zhores A. *Khrushchev: The Years in Power*. Translated by Andrew R. Durkin. New York: Columbia University Press, 1976.

Milburn, Thomas W. "The Management of Crisis." In *International Crises: Insights from Behavioral Research*, pp. 259–77. Edited by Charles F. Hermann. New York: The Free Press, 1972.

Miroff, Bruce. *Pragmatic Illusions: The Presidential Politics of John F. Kennedy*. New York: David McKay, 1976.

Neustadt, Richard E. *Presidential Power: The Politics of Leadership*. New York: John Wiley, 1960; "Afterword JFK," 1968.

————, and Allison, Graham T. "Afterword" to *Thirteen Days: A Memoir of the Cuban Missile Crisis* by Robert F. Kennedy. New York: W. W. Norton, 1971.

O'Donnell, Kenneth P.; Powers, David F.; and McCarthy, Joe. *Johnny, We Hardly Knew Ye: Memories of John Fitzgerald Kennedy*. Boston: Little, Brown, 1970.

Pachter, Henry M. *Collision Course: The Cuban Missile Crisis and Coexistence.* New York: Frederick A. Praeger, 1963.

Paper, Lewis J. *The Promise and the Performance: The Leadership of John F. Kennedy.* New York: Crown Publishers, 1975.

Penkovskiy, Oleg. *The Penkovskiy Papers.* Translated by Peter Deriabin. Garden City, N.Y.: Doubleday, 1965.

Perry, Robert L. *The Ballistic Missile Decisions.* Santa Monica, Calif.: RAND Corporation, 1967.

Rostow, Walt W. *The Diffusion of Power: An Essay in Recent History.* New York: Macmillan, 1972.

Russell, Bertrand R. *Unarmed Victory.* New York: Simon and Schuster, 1963.

Salinger, Pierre. *With Kennedy.* Garden City, N.Y.: Doubleday, 1966.

Scheinman, Lawrence, and Wilkinson, David, ed. *International Law and Political Crisis.* Boston: Little, Brown, 1968.

Schick, Jack M. *The Berlin Crisis.* Philadelphia: University of Pennsylvania Press, 1971.

Schlesinger, Arthur M., Jr. *A Thousand Days: John F. Kennedy in the White House.* Boston: Houghton Mifflin, 1965; paperback ed., Greenwich, Conn.: Fawcett Publications, 1966.

————. *Robert Kennedy and His Times.* Boston: Houghton Mifflin, 1978.

Schwab, Peter, and Scheidman, J. Lee. *John F. Kennedy.* New York: Twayne Publications, 1974.

Sidey, Hugh. *John F. Kennedy, President.* 2nd ed. New York: Atheneum, 1964.

Smith, Malcolm E., Jr. *Kennedy's Thirteen Greatest Mistakes in the White House.* New York: The National Forum of America, 1968.

Smith, Robert F. *What Happened in Cuba: A Documentary History.* New York: Twayne Publishers, 1963.

Sobel, Lester A., ed. *Cuba, the U.S. and Russia, 1960–1963: A Journalistic Narrative of Events in Cuba and of Cuban Relations with the U.S. and the Soviet Union.* New York: Facts on File, 1964.

Sorensen, Theodore C. *Decision Making in the White House: The Olive Branch or the Arrows.* New York: Columbia University Press, 1963.

————. *Kennedy.* New York: Harper and Row, 1965; paperback ed., New York: Bantam Books, 1966.

————. *The Kennedy Legacy.* New York: Macmillan, 1969.

Steel, Ronald. *Imperialists and Other Heroes: A Chronicle of the American Empire.* New York: Random House, 1971.

Stone, I. F. *In A Time of Torment.* New York: Random House, 1967.

Stone, Ralph A., ed. *John F. Kennedy: 1917–1963.* Dobbs Ferry, N.Y.: Oceana Publications, 1971.

Tatu, Michael. *Power in the Kremlin: From Khrushchev to Kosygin.* Translated by Helen Katel. New York: The Viking Press, 1969.

Taylor, Maxwell D. *Swords and Plowshares.* New York: W. W. Norton, 1972.

Thomas, Hugh. *Cuba: The Pursuit of Freedom.* New York: Harper and Row, 1971.

Ulam, Adam B. *Expansion and Coexistence: The History of Soviet Foreign Policy, 1917-1967.* New York: Praeger Publishers, 1968.

———. *The Rivals: America and Russia Since World War II.* New York: The Viking Press, 1971.

Walton, Richard J. *Cold War and Counterrevolution: The Foreign Policy of John F. Kennedy.* New York: The Viking Press, 1972.

———. *The United States and Latin America.* New York: Seabury Press, 1972.

Weintal, Edward, and Bartlett, Charles. *Facing the Brink: An Intimate Study of Crisis Diplomacy.* New York: Charles Scribner's Sons, 1967.

Wesson, Robert G. *Soviet Foreign Policy in Perspective.* Homewood, Ill.: The Dorsey Press, 1969.

Wicker, Tom. *Kennedy Without Tears: The Man Beneath the Myth.* New York: Morrow and Company, 1964.

Williams, William Appleton. *Some Presidents: Wilson to Nixon.* New York: Vintage Books, 1972.

Wohlstetter, Albert, and Wohlstetter, Robert. *Controlling the Risks in Cuba.* Adelphi Paper No. 17. London: Institute for Strategic Studies, 1965.

Wolfe, Thomas. *Soviet Strategy at the Crossroads.* Cambridge, Mass.: Harvard University Press, 1964.

Young, Oran R. *The Politics of Force: Bargaining During International Crises.* Princeton, N.J.: Princeton University Press, 1968.

ARTICLES

Acheson, Dean. "Dean Acheson's Version of Robert Kennedy's Version of the Cuban Missile Affair: Homage to Plain Dumb Luck." *Esquire,* February 1969, pp. 44, 46, 76–77.

Allison, Graham T. "Conceptual Models and the Cuban Missile Crisis." *American Political Science Review* 56 (September 1969): 689–718.

Alsop, Stewart, and Bartlett, Charles. "In Time of Crisis," *Saturday Evening Post,* December 8, 1962, pp. 16–20.

Anderson, Paul A. "Justifications and Precedents as Constraints in

Foreign Policy Decision-Making." *American Journal of Political Science* 25, no. 4 (1981): 738–61.

———. "Decision Making by Objection and the Cuban Missile Crisis." *Administrative Science Quarterly* 28 (June 1983): 201–22.

Bernstein, Barton J. "Courage and Commitment: The Missiles of October." *Foreign Service Journal* 52 (December 1975): 9–11, 24–27.

———. "The Cuban Missile Crisis: Trading the Jupiters in Turkey?" *Political Science Quarterly* 95 (Spring 1980): 97–125.

Bundy, McGeorge. "The Presidency and the Peace." *Foreign Affairs* 42 (April 1964): 353–65.

Caldwell, Dan. "A Research Note on the Quarantine of Cuba, October 1962." *International Studies Quarterly* 22 (December 1978): 625–33.

Carleton, William G. "Kennedy in History: An Early Appraisal." *The Antioch Review* 24 (Fall 1964): 277–99.

Crane, Robert D. "The Cuban Crisis: A Strategic Analysis of American and Soviet Policy." *Orbis* 6 (Winter 1963): 528–63.

———. "The Sino-Soviet Dispute on War and the Cuban Crisis." *Orbis* 7 (Fall 1 964): 537–49.

Dewart, Leslie. "The Cuban Crisis Revisited." *Studies on the Left* 5 (Spring 1965): 15–40.

Eckhardt, William, and White, Ralph K. "A Test of the Mirror-Image Hypothesis: Kennedy and Khrushchev." *Journal of Conflict Resolution* 11 (September 1967): 325–32.

Fenwick, Charles G. "The Quarantine Against Cuba: Legal or Illegal?" *American Journal of International Law* 57 (July 1963): 588–92.

Galbraith, John Kenneth. "Storm Over Havana: Who Were the Real Heroes?" *Chicago Tribune*, January 29, 1969, sec. 4, pp. 1, 16.

Garthoff, Raymond L. "American Reaction to Soviet Aircraft in Cuba, 1962 and 1978." *Political Science Quarterly* 95 (Fall 1980): 427–39.

———. "The Meaning of the Missiles." *Washington Quarterly* 5 (Autumn 1982): 76–82.

Hafner, Donald L. "Bureaucratic Politics and 'Those Frigging Missiles': JFK, Cuba and U.S. Missiles in Turkey." *Orbis* 21 (Summer 1977): 307–33.

Hagan, Roger. "Cuba: Triumph or Tragedy?" *Dissent* 10 (Winter 1963): 13–26.

———, and Bernstein, Bart. "Military Values of the Missiles in Cuba." *Bulletin of the Atomic Scientists* 19 (February 1963): 8–13.

Hargrove, Erwin C. "Presidential Personality and Revisionist Views of the Presidency." *American Journal of Political Science* 17 (November 1973): 819–35.

Hilsman, Roger. "The Cuban Missile Crisis: How Close We Were to War." *Look*, August 25, 1964, pp. 17–21.

———, and Steel, Ronald. "An Exchange on the Missile Crisis." *The New York Review of Books* 12 (May 8, 1969): 36–38.

Horelick, Arnold L. "The Cuban Missile Crisis: An Analysis of Soviet Calculations and Behavior." *World Politics* 16 (April 1964): 364–77.

Johns, Forrest R. "United We Stood." *United States Naval Institute Proceedings* III (1985): 78–84.

Kahan, Jerome H., and Long, Anne K. "The Cuban Missile Crisis: A Study of Its Strategic Context." *Political Science Quarterly* 87 (December 1972): 564–90.

Kateb, George. "Kennedy as Statesman." *Commentary* 41 (June 1966): 54–60.

Keating, Kenneth. "My Advance View of the Cuban Crisis." *Look*, November 3, 1964, pp. 96–106.

Kissinger, Henry A. "Reflections on Cuba." *The Reporter*, November 22, 1962, pp. 21–24.

Knorr, Klaus. "Failures in National Intelligence Estimates: The Case of the Cuban Missiles." *World Politics* 16 (April 1964): 455–67.

Knox, William E. "Close-Up of Khrushchev During a Crisis." *New York Times Magazine*, November 18, 1962, pp. 32, 128–29.

Krasner, Stephen D. "Are Bureaucracies Important? or Allison in Wonderland." *Foreign Policy* 7 (Summer 1976): 159–79.

Lebow, Richard N. "The Cuban Missile Crisis: Reading the Lessons Correctly." *Political Science Quarterly* 98 (Fall 1983): 431–58.

Licklider, Roy E. "The Missile Gap Controversy." *Political Science Quarterly* 85 (December 1970): 600–13.

Lockhart, Charles. "The Varying Fortunes of Increment Commitment: An Inquiry into the Cuban and Southeast Asian Cases." *International Studies Quarterly* 19 (March 1975): 46–66.

Lowenthal, David. "U.S. Cuban Policy: Illusion and Reality." *National Review*, January 29, 1963, pp. 61–63.

Lukas, J. Anthony. "Class Reunion: Kennedy's Men Relive the Cuban Missile Crisis." *New York Times Magazine*, August 30, 1987, pp. 22–27ff.

Meeker, Leonard C. "Defensive Quarantine and the Law." *American Journal of International Law* 57 (July 1963): 515–24.

Mongar, Thomas M. "Personality and Decision-Making: John F. Kennedy in Four Crisis Decisions." *Canadian Journal of Political Science* 2 (June 1969): 200–25.

Nathan, James A. "The Missile Crisis: His Finest Hour Now." *World Politics* 27 (January 1975): 256–81.

Nixon, Richard M. "Cuba, Castro and John F. Kennedy." *Reader's Digest*, November 1964, pp. 283–300.

Onuf, Nicholas G. "Law and Lawyers in International Crises." *International Organization* 29 (Autumn 1975): 1035–53.

Pachter, Henry M. "JFK as an Equestrian Statue: On Myth and Mythmakers." *Salmagundi* 1 (Spring 1966): 3–26.

Paterson, Thomas G. "Bearing the Burden: A Critical Look at JFK's Foreign Policy." *The Virginia Quarterly Review* 54 (Spring 1978): 193–212.

————., and Brophy, William J. "October Missiles and November Elections: the Cuban Missile Crisis and American Politics, 1962." *Journal of American History* 73 (June 1986): 87–120.

Pedersen, John C. "Soviet Reporting of the Cuban Crisis." *U.S. Naval Institute Proceedings* 91 (October 1965): 54–63.

Pollard, Robert A. "The Cuban Missile Crisis: Legacies and Lessons." *Military Review* 62 (Autumn 1982): 45–55.

Rodman, Peter W. "The Missiles of October: Twenty Years Later." *Commentary* 74 (October 1982): 39–46.

Rusk, Dean et al. "The Lessons of the Cuban Missile Crisis: Twentieth Anniversary of the Crisis." *Time*, September 27, 1982, pp. 85–86.

Scherer, John L. "Reinterpreting Soviet Behavior during the Cuban Missile Crisis." *World Affairs* 144 (Fall 1981): 110–25.

Sidey, Hugh. "The Presidency: The Classic Use of the Great Office." *Life*, November 22, 1968, p. 4.

Smith, Steve. "Allison and the Cuban Missile Crisis: A Review of the Bureaucratic Politics Model of Foreign Policy Decision-Making." *Journal of International Studies* 9, no. 1 (1980): 21–40.

Snyder, Jack L. "Rationality at the Brink: The Role of Cognitive Processes in the Failure of Deterrence." *World Politics* 30 (April 1978): 345–65.

Steel, Ronald. "Endgame." Review of *Thirteen Days* by Robert F. Kennedy. *The New York Review of Books* 12 (March 13, 1969): 15–22.

Stone, I. F. "The Brink." Review of *The Missile Crisis* by Elie Abel. *The New York Review of Books* 6 (April 14, 1966): 12–16.

Thorson, Stuart J., and Sylvan, Donald A. "Counterfactuals and the Cuban Missile Crisis." *International Studies Quarterly* 26, no. 4 (1982): 539–71.

Trachtenberg, Marc. "The Influence of Nuclear Weapons in the Cuban Missile Crisis." *International Security* 10 (Summer 1985): 137–63.

————. "White House Tapes and Minutes of the Cuban Missile Crisis:

ExCom Meetings, October 1962." *International Security* 10 (Summer 1985): 164–203.

Wills, Garry. "The Prisoner of Toughness." *Atlantic*, February 1982, pp. 52–67.

Wilson, Larman C. "International Law and the United States Cuban Quarantine of 1962." *Journal of Inter-American Studies* 7 (October 1965): 485–92.

Wohlstetter, Roberta. "Cuba and Pearl Harbor: Hindsight and Foresight." *Foreign Affairs* 43 (July 1965): 691–707.

INDEX

Abel, Elie, *The Missile Crisis*, 71-72

Accommodation, 82, 83, 84-85, 88, 95

Acheson, Dean, 5; "Dean Acheson's Version of Robert Kennedy's Version of the Cuban Missile Affair," 89-91

"Afterword: JFK" (Neustadt), 67-68

Air Force Reserve, 26

Air strike: contingency plans for, 21–22; debate over, 7; potential for, 5; preparations for, 25; problems with, 38, 40; support for, 6, 43-44, 90, 91, 143

Allison, Graham T., 68

Alsop, Stewart, "In Time of Crisis," 64-65

Anderson, George W., Jr., 8

Anderson, Rudolf, Jr., 2, 25, 141

Arms limitations, 27

Arms race, 104, 117, 121, 147

Balance of power, 100, 133; appearance of, 35, 55, 66; and buildup, 36, 37-38, 53; change in, 49, 64, 75, 84, 86, 90, 94, 135; political versus strategic, 65, 109-10, 118-19, 141; and prestige, 103; strategic, 131, 143

Ball, George, 9

Bartlett, Charles, *Facing the Brink*, 73; "In Time of Crisis," 64-65

Bay of Pigs, 84, 91, 92, 94, 108, 116, 118

"Bearing the Burden" (Paterson), 117-18

Beggs, Robert, *The Cuban Missile Crisis*, 107

Berlin issue, 5-6, 106

Berlin Wall, 84, 91, 94

Bernstein, Barton J., 121-22; "The Cuban Missile Crisis," 113–14

Bethel, Paul D., *The Losers*, 92-94

Blockade: as act of war, 16; confirmation of, 8; dangers of, 116; debate over, 7; effectiveness of, 19, 39; evolution of, 69; and international law, 51-52; media treatment of, 131-32;

Blockade (*continued*)
   military initiation of, 8; as military response, 144; as nonpolitical measure, 46; political
   purpose of, 66; potential for, 5;
   problems with, 74, 90; proclamation of, 16-17; public justification for, 52; support for, 5,
   6, 38-39, 40; termination of, 30
"Brink, The" (Stone), 104-5
Brinkmanship, 63, 64, 71, 75,
   135-36
Bucharest (tanker), 19, 47, 53-54
Buildup: alarm over, 1; defensive
   versus offensive, 101, 108, 114,
   119, 143; evidence of, 2-3, 4, 5,
   20; Ex Com theories of, 36;
   left-wing explanation of, 101,
   106, 107, 109, 115, 119; motives
   for, 141-42; potential responses
   to, 4, 143-44; progress of, 21,
   25; as psychological victory,
   143; right-wing explanation of,
   84, 87, 90, 94; Soviet explanation for, 1, 57 n.6, 127-28, 129;
   Sovietologist explanation for,
   129-30, 131, 132, 134, 135, 136;
   traditionalist explanation of,
   43, 45-46, 49, 50-51, 52-53, 55,
   64, 67, 73
Bundy, McGeorge, 3; air strike
   scenario, 7; on buildup, 2;
   "The Presidency and the
   Peace," 42

Carleton, William G., "Kennedy
   in History: An Early Appraisal,"
   66-67
Carroll, Joseph, 3
Carter, Marshall, 3
Castro, Fidel, 29, 49, 50, 82, 85,
   86, 87

Central Intelligence Agency
   (CIA), 3
Chayes, Abram, *The Cuban Mis-
   sile Crisis,* 51-52
China, 132-33
Clinch, Nancy Gager, 110-12, *The
   Kennedy Neurosis,* 110-12
Cline, Ray, 3
Coercion, 83
Cold War, 48; change in, 65, 134;
   strengthening of, 115; thaw in,
   36; traditionalist theory of, 37-
   38
Cold War and Counterrevolution
   (Walton), 107-9
Collision Course (Pachter), 70
Conciliation, 81
Confrontation, versus diplo-
   macy, 47, 99, 106, 110, 111,
   114, 118, 120, 144, 145
Crane, Robert D., "The Cuban
   Crisis: A Strategic Analysis of
   American and Soviet Policy,"
   83-85
Crisis management, 75
Cuba, abandonment of, 92, 93,
   95
"Cuba, Castro and John F. Ken-
   nedy" (Nixon), 83
"Cuba: Triumph or Tragedy?"
   (Hagan), 100-101
"Cuban Crisis, The: A Strategic
   Analysis of American and So-
   viet Policy" (Crane), 83-85
"Cuban Crisis Revisited, The"
   (Dewart), 101-3
Cuban missile crisis: as decep-
   tion, 93-94, 102; distinct fea-
   tures of, 47-48; importance of,
   68-69, 147-48; as Kremlin vic-
   tory, 83; left-wing view of, 99-
   100, 104, 115, 117, 118-21; and

press credibility, 53-54; resolution of, 29-30; right-wing view of, 81-82, 85, 86-87, 89, 92, 94-96; Sovietologists' view of, 137; traditionalist view of, 39-40, 48, 51, 56, 67; U.S. political implications of, 40. *See also* Blockade; Buildup

Cuban Missile Crisis, The (Beggs), 107

"Cuban Missile Crisis, The" (Bernstein), 113-14

Cuban Missile Crisis, The (Chayes), 51-52

"Cuban Missile Crisis, 1962, The" (George), 73-75

"Cuban Missile Crisis, The: A Study of Its Strategic Context" (Kahan and Long), 134-35

Dagger in the Heart (Lazo), 91-92

Daniel, James, *Strike in the West*, 85-87

"Dean Acheson's Version of Robert Kennedy's Version of the Cuban Missile Affair" (Acheson), 89-91

Decade of Disillusionment (Heath), 114-15

de Gaulle, Charles, 147

Détente, 36, 48, 56, 67

Dewart, Leslie, "The Cuban Crisis Revisited," 101-3

Diffusion of Power, The (Rostow), 50-51

Dinerstein, Herbert S., *The Making of a Missile Crisis*, 135-36

Diplomacy, 73-74, 75; versus confrontation, 47, 99, 106, 110, 111, 114, 118, 120, 144, 145

Dobrynin, Anatoly, 5, 28, 41, 146

"Endgame" (Steel), 105-7

England, U.S. missiles in, 89, 115

Escalation, 41, 100

Executive Committee (Ex Com): air strike/invasion contingency plans, 21; alternative responses to buildup, 38; and blockade decision, 55-56; buildup theories of, 36; evaluation of, 90-91; internal workings of, 40; manipulation of, 93; meeting schedule of, 9; membership, 3-4; on postsecret letter communiqué, 25; on secret letter, 24

Facing the Brink (Weintal and Bartlett), 73

Fairlie, Henry, *The Kennedy Promise*, 112-13

First-strike capability, 5, 100, 114

FitzSimons, Louise, *The Kennedy Doctrine*, 109-10

Flexible response, 48

Fomin, Aleksander, 22, 26

Free World Colossus, The (Horowitz), 103-4

Gagarin (ship), 17

Galbraith, John Kenneth, 122-23 n.30

Garcia-Inchaustegui, 16

George, Alexander L., "The Cuban Missile Crisis, 1962," 73-75

Gilpatric, Roswell, 3

Gromyko, Anatolii, 57 n.6; *Through Russian Eyes*, 127, 128-29

Gromyko, Andrei, 5, 6

Guantanamo Bay, 8

Hagan, Roger, 121-22, n.4;
"Cuba: Triumph or Tragedy?,"
100-101
Heath, Jim F., *Decade of Disillusionment*, 114-15
Hilsman, Roger, 3, 9, 22; *To Move a Nation*, 48-50
Horelick, Arnold L., *Strategic Power and Soviet Foreign Policy*, 129
Horowitz, David, *The Free World Colossus*, 103-4
Hot line, 36, 48, 56
Hubbell, John, *Strike in the West*, 85-87

Intercontinental ballistic missiles (ICBMs), 8
Intermediate-range ballistic missiles (IRBMs), 5, 8
International law, 51-52
"In Time of Crisis" (Alsop and Bartlett), 64-65
Invasion: contingency plans for, 22; preparations for, 25-26; problems with, 40; support for, 143
Italy, U.S. missiles in, 7, 64, 88, 89, 109, 115, 128

John F. Kennedy, President (Sidey), 65-66
Johnny, We Hardly Knew Ye (O'Donnell), 52-53
Johnson, Alexis, 7
Joint Chiefs of Staff: on air strike, 6; air strike/invasion preference, 25; blockade plan initiation, 8; meeting with Kennedy, 9; and troop movements, 5

Kahan, Jerome H., "The Cuban Missile Crisis: A Study of Its Strategic Context," 134-35
Keating, Kenneth, 2, 88
Kennedy, John F.: Attorney General's evaluation of, 41-42; blockade proclamation, 16-17; on campaign tour, 4, 7; as Cold War warrior, 109, 112; and communication to Khrushchev, 9, 17, 18; crisis behavior of, 145; decision-making of, 46-47; and full alert order, 25-26; initial buildup response, 1, 2, 9; left-wing evaluation of, 108, 119-21; and Gromyko, 5-6; national address by, 9-10; neurosis of, 111, 112; and nuclear war, 112, 113; observers' evaluation of, 63-64, 66-67, 68, 69, 70, 71, 72, 74-75, 76; participants' evaluation of, 36, 39, 44, 48, 50, 53, 54, 56, 63; political motivations of, 95, 99, 100, 103-4, 105, 106, 110, 145; and power, 113, 117-18; prestige needs of, 104, 105, 107-8, 109, 110, 115, 116-17, 120; right-wing evaluation of, 73, 81-82, 83-84, 87-89, 91-92, 95; and secret letter, 23-24, 27
Kennedy, Robert F.: as Assistant President, 93; on blockade, 40; meeting with Dobrynin, 28, 41, 146; and secret letter, 27; *Thirteen Days*, 40-42
Kennedy (Sorensen), 36-40, 129
Kennedy Doctrine, The (Fitz-Simons), 109-10
"Kennedy in History: An Early Appraisal" (Carleton), 66-67
Kennedy Neurosis, The (Clinch), 110-12

Kennedy Promise, The (Fairlie), 112-13

Kennedy's Thirteen Greatest Mistakes in the White House (Smith), 88-89

Khrushchev, Nikita: assurances from, 6; on blockade, 18; buildup justification, 127-28; and buildup legality, 51; communication with, 9, 17, 18; and crisis termination, 47; final crisis communiqué, 28-29; initial response of, 15; *Khrushchev Remembers,* 57 n.6, 127, 137 n.1; left-wing praise of, 121; postsecret letter communiqué, 24-25, 70-71; as realist, 65; secret letter from, 23-24, 70-71, 132

Khrushchev Remembers (Khrushchev), 57. n.6, 127, 137 n.1

Knox, William E., 18

Komiles (ship), 17

Lane, Thomas A., *The Leadership of President Kennedy,* 87-88

Laos, neutralization of, 84, 91, 94

Launch pads, 5, 21

Lazo, Mario, *Dagger in the Heart,* 91-92

Leadership of President Kennedy, The (Lane), 87-88

Lens, Sidney, 124 n.66

Lippmann, Walter, 18-19

Long, Anne K., "The Cuban Missile Crisis: A Study of Its Strategic Context," 134-35

Losers, The (Bethel), 92-94

Lowenthal, David, "U.S. Cuban Policy: Illusion or Reality," 82-83

McNamara, Robert, 3; on blockade, 40

Making of a Missile Crisis, The (Dinerstein), 135-36

Malinovsky, R. Y., 15

Marucla (ship), 21

Medium-range ballistic missiles: base for, 2; range of, 4; sites for, 5; on Soviet targets, 8

Military Air Transport Command, 8

Miroff, Bruce, *Pragmatic Illusions,* 115-17

Missile Crisis, The (Abel), 71-72

Missile gap, 37, 89

Missiles: defensive versus offensive, 101, 108, 114, 119, 143; detection delay, 43; sites for, 5. *See also* specific types

Monroe Doctrine, 51, 87, 88-89, 90

National Security Council (NSC), 3; meeting with Kennedy, 7, 9. *See also* Executive Committee

Neustadt, Richard E., "Afterword: JFK," 67-68

Nixon, Richard M., "Cuba, Castro and John F. Kennedy," 83

North Atlantic Treaty Organization (NATO), 16, 121

Nuclear confrontation, blueprint for, 68, 76

Nuclear paradox, 68-69

Nuclear test ban treaty, 36, 40, 48, 56, 67, 89, 100, 117

Nuclear war, 124 n.66; probability of, 48, 87-88, 107, 109, 112, 113, 146, 147; responsibility for, 69-70

O'Donnell, Kenneth P., *Johnny, We Hardly Knew Ye,* 52-53

Organization of American States (OAS), 8, 16, 50, 51

Pachter, Henry M., *Collision Course*, 70
Paterson, Thomas G., "Bearing the Burden," 117-18
Peaceful coexistence, 39-40, 56, 67
Power in the Kremlin (Tatu), 130-32
Pragmatic Illusions (Miroff), 115-17
Pravda, 21, 131-32
"Presidency and the Peace, The" (Bundy), 42
Pruessen, Ronald, *Reflections on the Cold War*, 113

Quarantine. *See* Blockade

Rapprochement, 93, 95
Reflections on the Cold War (Pruessen), 113
Republicans, 1
Rivals, The (Ulam), 132-34
Robert Kennedy and His Times (Schlesinger), 45
Rostow, Walt W., *The Diffusion of Power*, 50-51
Rush, Myron, *Strategic Power and Soviet Foreign Policy*, 129
Rusk, Dean, 3, 15-16, 22

Salinger, Pierre, 7; *With Kennedy*, 53-54
San Cristobal, Cuba, 3
Sanctions, economic, 2
Scali, John, 22, 26
Schlesinger, Arthur M., Jr.: *Robert Kennedy and His Times*, 45; *A Thousand Days*, 45-48
Second-strike capability, 100, 114
Secrecy, 4, 11, 21, 101
Security, 128

Sidey, Hugh, *John F. Kennedy, President*, 65-66
Smith, Malcolm E., *Kennedy's Thirteen Greatest Mistakes in the White House*, 88-89
Sorensen, Theodore, 7; *Kennedy*, 36-40, 129
Soviet intelligence, 45, 132; miscalculations by, 35, 49, 54, 55, 64, 72, 75, 142
Soviet Union: armed forces in, 15; and blockade, 39; and China, 132-33; concessions from, 22, 29-30; and nuclear superiority, 89, 104; retreat by, 49-50, 56, 65, 128, 132, 136-37, 146
Steel, Ronald, "Endgame," 105-7
Stevenson, Adlai, 10, 64; debate with Zorin, 20; before United Nations, 16; on U.S. concessions, 7-8
Stone, I. F., "The Brink," 104-5
Strategic Air Command, 4
Strategic Power and Soviet Foreign Policy (Horelick and Rush), 129-30
Surface-to-air missiles (SAMs), 2-3
Sweeney, Walter C., Jr., 8
Swords and Plowshares (Taylor), 42-45

Tactical Air Command, 8, 44
Tass news agency, 15
Tatu, Michael, *Power in the Kremlin*, 130-32
Taylor, Maxwell D., 3, 6; *Swords and Plowshares*, 42-45
Thirteen Days (Kennedy, R. F.), 40-42

Thousand Days, A (Schlesinger), 45-48

Through Russian Eyes (Gromyko), 127, 128-29

To Move a Nation (Hilsman), 48-50

Trollope Ploy, 27, 64

Turkey: as crisis bargaining point, 7, 19, 26, 41, 64, 109, 111, 116, 128; U.S. missiles in, 58 n.30, 71, 101, 115; U.S. withdrawal from, 88, 89

Ulam, Adam B., *The Rivals*, 132-34

United Nations, 8, 52

United Nations Security Council, 10-11

United States, concessions from, 83, 109, 128

"U.S. Cuban Policy: Illusion or Reality" (Lowenthal), 82-83

United States intelligence: complacency of, 65; failures of, 43; miscalculations of, 35, 45, 49, 54-55, 64; 72, 75, 85, 142; mishandling of, 106

United States Intelligence Board, 5

U.S.S. *Joseph P. Kennedy, Jr.*, 21

U Thant, 19-20, 21

U-2 incident, 26, 47, 147

U-2 reconnaissance flights, 2, 4, 21, 128, 146

Vietnam, 100, 117, 121

Walton, Richard J., *Cold War and Counterrevolution*, 107-9

War psychology, 67

Warsaw Pact, 15

Weintal, Edward, *Facing the Brink*, 73

West Berlin, 37

Western Hemisphere, Soviet intrusion into, 53, 82, 83, 116

White, Lincoln, 22, 47

With Kennedy (Salinger), 53-54

Zorin, Valerian, 11, 16, 20

ABOUT THE AUTHOR

WILLIAM J. MEDLAND is Professor of American History and Executive Vice President/Provost at Saint Mary's College of Minnesota. He is a graduate of the University of Notre Dame and received M.A.s in history and adult education and a Ph.D. in social science (American history) from Ball State University. He also has studied at the Graduate School of Saint Louis University, Harvard University, and the Center for Security Studies of the University of Wisconsin, Madison.

Since 1967 Dr. Medland has been a teacher and an academic administrator in several midwestern colleges and universities. He has authored articles and monographs both in history and education. His research interest is the United States in the nuclear age. He teaches a popular multidisciplinary course to college seniors on this topic that involves faculty from the disciplines of biology, history, military science, philosophy, physics, political science, psychology, and theology.

Medland is active in many professional and educational organizations. He currently is a consultant-evaluator for the Commission on Institutions of Higher Education of the North Central Association.